Bab Animals

Activity Book

Name _____

Age _____

Class _____

OXFORD
UNIVERSITY PRESS

OXFORD
UNIVERSITY PRESS

Great Clarendon Street, Oxford OX2 6DP

Oxford University Press is a department of the University of Oxford.
It furthers the University's objective of excellence in research, scholarship,
and education by publishing worldwide in

Oxford New York

Auckland Bangkok Buenos Aires Cape Town Chennai
Dar es Salaam Delhi Hong Kong Istanbul Karachi Kolkata
Kuala Lumpur Madrid Melbourne Mexico City Mumbai
Nairobi São Paulo Shanghai Taipei Tokyo Toronto

OXFORD and OXFORD ENGLISH are registered trade marks of
Oxford University Press in the UK and in certain other countries

© Oxford University Press 2005

The moral rights of the author have been asserted

Database right Oxford University Press (maker)

First published 2005

2009 2008 2007 2006 2005

10 9 8 7 6 5 4 3 2 1

ISBN 13: 978 0 19 440143 2
ISBN 10: 0 19 440143 X

Printed in China

Activities by: Rebecca Brooke
Illustrations by: Genny Haines
Original story by: Richard Northcott

Connect.

gorilla •

rabbit •

sheep •

cat •

dog •

lion •

1

Connect.

kitten

lamb

cub

baby gorilla

puppy

1

2

3

4

5

Circle.

1 What is a baby dog?

a kitten   a lamb   (a puppy)

2 What is a mother kitten?

a dog   a sheep   a cat

3 What animal is small?

an elephant   an ant   a dog

4 What animal is big?

an ant   a kitten

an elephant

5 What animal is cute?

a puppy   a banana   an ant

Write.

two   three   five   six

❶ How many white puppies?
   two

❷ How many brown and white puppies? _____

❸ How many brown puppies?

   _____

❹ How many black and white puppies? _____

❺ How many gray puppies?

   _____

Write.

sheep   lamb   ~~kitten~~
dog   rabbit

1  kitten

2

3

4

5

Write.

dog   kitten   sheep
eyes   ears   noses

❶ A baby _sheep_ is a lamb.

❷ Rabbits have two long

_____ .

❸ A baby cat is a _____ .

❹ A baby _____ is a puppy.

❺ The rabbits have pink

_____ .

❻ The rabbits have black

_____ .

Circle yes or no .

1. Baby sheep are lambs. (yes) no

2. Baby lions are kittens. yes no

3. Rabbits have long ears. yes no

4. Baby lions are cubs. yes no

5. Rabbits have two noses. yes no

6. Lion cubs like to play. yes no

7. The lion has three cubs. yes no

Write the names.

gorilla   lion   baby gorilla   cubs

❶ They like to play. ____cubs____

❷ He loves his father.

_____

❸ She has two cubs. _____

❹ He is on his father's back.

_____

❺ She is brown and white.

_____

❻ He is big and black.

_____

Write.

one	two

1 How many blue kittens?

two

2 How many black kittens?

_____

3 How many white kittens?

_____

4 How many brown and white puppies? _____

5 How many black and white puppies? _____

Connect.

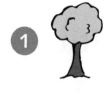

1

bird

2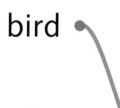

gorilla

3

lion

4

cub

baby gorilla

5

tree

6

Circle yes **or** no .

1. The lion has
   three cubs.   yes no

2. The dog has
   five puppies.   yes no

3. The sheep has
   four lambs.   yes no

4. The gorilla has
   six babies.   yes no

5. The cat has
   one kitten.   yes no

6. The kitten is cute.   yes no

Connect.

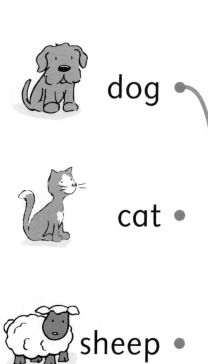

dog

lamb

cat

baby gorilla

sheep

puppy

gorilla

cub

lion

kitten

Look and write.

Chant.

What is a baby dog?

A baby dog is a puppy.

What is a baby cat?

A baby cat is a kitten.

What are baby sheep?

Baby sheep are lambs.

What are baby lions?

Baby lions are cubs.

CW00894033

CHELSEA F.C.

– THE 25 YEAR RECORD

1971-72 to 1995-96 Seasons

SEASON BY SEASON WRITE-UPS
David Powter

EDITOR
Michael Robinson

CONTENTS

British Library Cataloguing in Publication Data
A catalogue record for this book is available from the British Library
ISBN 0-947808-77-9

Copyright © 1996; SOCCER BOOK PUBLISHING LTD. (01472-696226)
72, St. Peters' Avenue, Cleethorpes, N.E. Lincolnshire, DN35 8HU, England

Printed by Redwood Books, Kennet House, Kennet Way, Trowbridge, Wilts.

CHELSEA
– Seasons 1971-72 to 1995-96

Although Chelsea fans experienced the disappointment of losing manager Glenn Hoddle to the England set-up at the end of 1995-96, they were quickly buoyed by the news that his replacement was to be the eloquent Ruud Gullit as player-coach. The experienced Dutchman had ignited the Blues on the pitch in 1995-96 – his first season in England – and the thought of him also pulling the strings off the field filled the fans with great optimism.

There was also much anticipation at the club a quarter of a century earlier as Dave Sexton's Chelsea opened the 1971-72 campaign having won trophies (F.A. Cup and European Cup Winners' Cup) in each of the previous two seasons. Disappointingly, and despite some near misses, the club was to fail to add any more major trophies in the 25 seasons that followed.

The Blues opened their defence of the Cup Winners' Cup with a record 21-0 aggregate victory over Luxembourg outfit Jeunesse Hautcharage. Thirteen of those goals (5 by Peter Osgood) rattled into the Stamford Bridge nets, yet they later wished they had saved a few up for second round opponents Atvidaberg. Chelsea appeared in control when they secured a goalless draw on their travels in the first leg, but the Swedish side pulled off a major surprise by earning a 1-1 draw in London, to take the tie on the away goals rule.

Blackpool (away) and Bolton (home) were defeated as the Blues mounted another F.A. Cup campaign; but the bandwagon came to a juddering halt in the mud at Brisbane Road – the home of Second Division Orient. It all seemed to be going so well when Chelsea strode into a 2-0 lead, but it was the East Londoners who coped best with the quagmire conditions, scoring three times to send their ex-manager's side slithering out of the competition.

However, Chelsea did reach Wembley in 1972, when they battled through to the final of the League Cup. Replays were required at both the third and fourth round stages. Nottingham Forest were eventually beaten 2-1 at the Bridge, while Bolton's sturdy resistance (which earned a draw in London) crumbled as the Blues fired in six goals at Burnden Park. After defeating Norwich by a single goal away, Chelsea reached the final by edging past Spurs 5-4 on aggregate in a two-legged semi-final. The Londoners were the favourites at Wembley but succumbed to Stoke City and their veteran midfielder George

Eastham. The Potters won 2-1 to secure their first major trophy; Osgood netted Chelsea's goal.

The Blues' final League position of seventh masked many high quality performances. They collected only three wins from the first 13 games and finished by winning just one of their last six; but in between showed Championship-winning form (just 3 defeats in 23 games). Chelsea finished only ten points behind Champions Derby County, Osgood top scoring with 19.

Sexton's side started 1972-73 in positive fashion, beating Leeds, the previous term's runners-up, 4-0 at Stamford Bridge on the opening day and then following up seven days later by defeating the Champions at the Baseball Ground. The Blues could not maintain this form and, although they were still fifth at Christmas, finished 12th. They would have plummeted even lower if they had not won their final three games.

A shortage of goals (only 49 in total throughout the League campaign) and the distraction of two cup runs appeared to be the major reasons for their decline. Yet, there was again to be no glory on the cup fronts. Having defeated Derby en route to the League Cup semi-finals, Chelsea were favourites to reach their second successive final. However, relegation strugglers Norwich exacted their revenge for the previous year's exit by surprisingly winning both legs.

The Blues reached the sixth round of the F.A. Cup – sidestepping high flying Ipswich along the way – but their challenge was again to peter out on the other side of London, when Arsenal defeated them in a replay at Highbury.

With the board channelling most of its resources into constructing a huge new grandstand, Sexton was unable to stiffen the playing squad. The 1973-74 campaign started disastrously with three successive defeats and the Blues stayed stuck in a low gear all term. There was to be no joy in either cup competition and, mid-season, they lost Osgood (to Southampton) and Alan Hudson (to Stoke) – two of their biggest stars – after a public falling out with Sexton. With only two points gained from the last five games, they fell within one point of the Second Division in 17th place.

After seven years at the helm, Sexton was sacked the following October and former Scunthorpe and Blackpool boss Ron Suart stepped out of the Stamford Bridge shadows to become manager. With the odds stacked against him, he just failed to stop the club falling into the Second Division. They finished 21st, one point behind 'safe' Spurs. Their fate was sealed when they only won one of the final dozen fixtures. The Blues won just nine League games in 1974-75, with

Ian Hutchinson's meagre seven goals (out of a paltry tally of 42) proving good enough to make him the top scorer.

Suart stepped up to become General Manager two weeks before Chelsea were relegated, with coach and former left-back Eddie McCreadie taking charge of team affairs.

McCreadie's men made a mediocre start to their 1975-76 Second Division campaign by winning only two of the first 12 games. They improved slightly but a phenomenal 18 draws anchored them to finish 11th. Lack of fire-power was still a problem; they netted just 53 times, ever-present Ray Wilkins top scoring on the 11 goal mark.

Fourth Division Crewe spun Chelsea out of the League Cup; while hopes of 1975-76 F.A. Cup glory evaporated in the fifth round, when third-flight Crystal Palace won 3-2 at the Bridge.

Chelsea's absence from the First Division lasted just two years as McCreadie led them to promotion as runners-up in 1976-77. They lost only three times in the first half of the season and led the table for over six months from the end of September. However, Wolves sneaked in front as the Blues lost three times in a busy April. Chelsea still had a chance to take the title when they visited Molineux in the penultimate fixture; but although Tommy Langley gave the Londoners a first half lead, Wolves restored parity and went on to take the title by two points.

Having a settled side was one of the main ingredients for Chelsea's success. All of the team that appeared in the opening day victory (at Orient) went on to make 26 or more appearances. They included ever-presents Ray Wilkins, Gary Locke and Ray Lewington, together with keeper Peter Bonetti, Garry Stanley, Steve Wicks, David Hay (the club's record signing from Celtic), Ian Britton, Ken Swain, Graham Wilkins and top scorer Steve Finnieston (with 24 out of a total of 73).

Despite that healthy goalscoring record, the old problem of a lack of fire-power hindered the Blues back in the First Division in 1977-78. They never rose higher than 13th and finished 16th, four points above the relegation zone. Langley top scored, with 11 out of 46.

The Blues fell at the first hurdle at Anfield in the League Cup, but exacted revenge on Liverpool in the F.A. Cup by beating them 4-2 at the Bridge. However, after defeating Burnley 6-2, they stumbled out on their own ground to Orient (again) in a fifth round replay.

5

A dispute over contractual terms meant that the club had to replace McCreadie, who resigned in July 1978. They again looked within and promoted their youth team manager – and one of McCreadie's former full-back partners – Ken Shellito.

1978-79 proved to be a great disappointment for Chelsea fans. Shellito inherited a lot of players past their sell-by-date and, even worse, too many others who were not good enough for top-flight football. The Blues already looked good relegation bets – winning just two of their first 18 fixtures – when Shellito resigned after little more than five months in the job, on 13th December.

Coach Frank Upton's spell as caretaker lasted one day (enough to oversee the transfer of Swain to Aston Villa) before Daily Express football writer Danny Blanchflower was appointed manager. The former Spurs and Northern Ireland skipper (who had been detached from direct football affairs for 15 years) was soon in no doubt about the magnitude of his task, as within three days his side had crashed 7-2 at Middlesbrough. Peter Osgood had netted the Blues' first goal at Ayresome Park on his 'return' debut, but went on to score only once more for the club. Blanchflower went one better than Shellito by leading Chelsea to three wins in 1978-79, but it was never going to be good enough to pull them clear of relegation and they finished in 22nd and bottom place with just 20 points.

Bonetti (who retired after 600 League games) and Ray Wilkins (sold to Manchester United for a club record fee of £825,000) played their last games for Chelsea at the end of 1978-79. Then, the following September, Blanchflower resigned saying: "I always said I would go when the time was right. I think the moment has come. The club now need to appoint a younger man more in touch with the values of the game – particularly off the field." A younger man – coach Geoff Hurst – did take over. He was originally appointed caretaker, but after five successive victories he was made manager.

The 1979-80 Second Division title appeared to be a distinct possibility before the Blues stumbled and collected just two points from four crucial games in early April. They fought back to gain five points from their last three fixtures; but were shaded out of third place (and promotion) by Birmingham on goal difference, two points behind Champions Leicester City and one point behind runners-up Sunderland. Clive Walker top scored (with 13); while Ron Harris made his 655th and last League appearance – a club record.

Chelsea failed to win any of the first five matches of 1980-81, but found their form to move into the promotion reckoning by winning eleven of their next 14.

However, disaster then stuck Hurst's side as they only won three of their last 23 League games, netting just nine times! The 1966 World Cup final hat-trick hero must have wished he was able to field himself as, incredibly, his side scored in only three of the last 22 games. They did not score at all away from the Bridge after 29th November. Amazingly, the Blues were still a top six side as late as the end of March. But after failing to score in the last nine fixtures, they finished 12th.

With John Neal replacing Hurst as manager, Chelsea also finished 12th twelve months later. They faded out of the 1981-82 promotion picture by losing six times in a seven game spell in February and March. Hopes of F.A. Cup glory were crushed by Spurs in a Stamford Bridge quarter-final. The Blues had reached that stage by beating Liverpool 2-0 on the same pitch. Neal's side also defeated Southampton, another top-flight side, in the League Cup but then crashed out 4-2 at Fourth Division Wigan in the third round. In April 1982 Chelsea were bought by Ken Bates, who soon afterwards became the club's chairman.

Chelsea registered their worst ever League finish of 18th in Division Two in 1982-83, but stopped the rot just in time by staying unbeaten in the last four games. Thus they avoided a first taste of Third Division football by two points.

Neal brought in fresh blood and it paid off with the 1983-84 Second Division title. Former Reading striker Kerry Dixon was the Division's top scorer (with 28 goals), while also ever-present Eddie Niedzwiecki kept 17 clean sheets in the first season after his transfer from Neal's old club Wrexham. Other new signings Nigel Spackman, Joe McLaughlin and Pat Nevin made significant contributions, as did John Hollins who returned to the club from Arsenal. The other key squad members were Colin Pates, John Bumstead, Colin Lee, David Speedie, Joey Jones and Mickey Thomas (the latter pair also being ex-Wrexham players).

They ended on a high note, with a 17 game unbeaten run, winning each of their last four matches to edge the title on goal difference from Sheffield Wednesday.

With the experienced Doug Rougvie adding granite to the back four and Dixon following up with another 24 goals to be the First Division's joint top scorer (earning him a call-up to the England squad), Chelsea finished 1984-85 in an excellent sixth position in the First Division – their highest for 14 years.

Millwall, Walsall and Manchester City were all beaten in the Milk Cup en route to a home quarter-final with Sheffield Wednesday. The original meeting ended

1-1, and the replay also ended all-square at a frantic 4-4; but it was the Owls who flew into the semi-final with a 3-2 second replay victory, at Stamford Bridge.

John Hollins stepped up from player-coach to become manager in June 1985, after Neal underwent heart surgery. The former boss stayed on at the club in an advisory capacity.

Hollins's side also finished sixth in 1985-86, and would have been better placed but for losing their last four games. Dixon and Speedie both netted 14 times to be joint top scorers. Milk Cup glory looked a possibility after they battled through to the quarter-final stage. However, West London rivals QPR knocked them out in a Stamford Bridge replay.

Chelsea did win one competition in 1985-86 when they defeated Manchester City, 5-4, in the Full Members' Cup final at Wembley.

A dire start of just three wins from their 20 fixtures left them rock bottom at Christmas 1986, but five wins from the next seven helped them to finish 14th in 1986-87. There was also disappointment in the Littlewoods Cup, with their early exit being at the hands of Fourth Division Cardiff City.

Chelsea made a much better start to 1987-88, but by 22nd March had fallen from sixth to 17th place after going 18 games without winning. As a consequence, Hollins left the club by mutual consent and was replaced by coach Bobby Campbell. The fourth match afterwards brought a little relief with a home victory over Derby; but it failed to stop them eventually finishing 18th – in a play-off position. All told, the Blues won just one of the last 26 fixtures.

Some confidence seeped back into the side when they comfortably saw off Blackburn in the play-off semi finals. A 2-0 win, in the first leg, at Ewood Park was followed by a 4-1 margin at the Bridge. However, the Blues slipped up against the final Second Division opponents Middlesbrough. The Teesiders won the first leg 2-0 and, in London, Campbell's side could only muster a Gordon Durie effort and were relegated 2-1 on aggregate. Chelsea are the only side in modern times to lose their top-flight status via the play-off system.

Undaunted, the Blues bounced back at the first attempt, netting 96 goals to take the Second Division Championship. Although they did not head the table until Boxing Day, Chelsea only lost five times (once in the last 33 games), vaulting over the rest of the Division to finish a massive 17 points clear of runners-up Manchester City, with a club record 99 points.

Dixon was the main marksman with 25 goals, while Durie added another 17.

The other major contributions in 1988-89 came from McLaughlin, Bumstead, Clive Wilson, Peter Nicholas, Kevin McAllister, Tony Dorigo, Kevin Wilson, Steve Clarke, and the only ever-present, Graham Roberts. Dave Beasant's mid-season arrival from Newcastle added more assurance between the sticks.

There was to be no Littlewoods Cup run in 1988-89, Chelsea exiting at the first hurdle to Fourth Division Scunthorpe. Twelve months later, it was another basement side Scarborough who knocked Chelsea out of the same competition. In the F.A. Cup, the West Londoners made a fourth round exit at Third Division Bristol City.

Conversely, Campbell's side were very consistent in the League on their return to the top-flight in 1989-90. They made a fine start and led the table in mid November. Their one poor spell followed, when they failed to win in six fixtures and lost 5-2 at home to both Wimbledon and Liverpool, with a 4-2 defeat at QPR sandwiched in between. It was still a very creditable performance to finish in fifth place. Dixon top scored with 20 goals and Kevin Wilson contributed a further 14. The club did win a competition in 1989-90 – the ZDS Cup, beating Middlesbrough 1-0 in a Wembley final.

Chelsea won only three of the first 13 games of the following campaign, before five successive wins lifted them into top half of the table. They faded to finish 11th in 1990-91, with 12 goal Durie heading the scorers' list. However, they did have the distinction of inflicting the only League defeat in Champions Arsenal's record-breaking season.

The Blues were beaten 3-1 by Oxford United in the third round of the F.A. Cup; but the Second Division side were one of four opponents sidestepped en route to the Rumblelows Cup semi-final. Their best performance was in defeating Spurs 3-0 in a White Hart Lane quarter-final replay. However, Sheffield Wednesday proved to be stiff opposition in the last four and the second Division side won both legs by two goal margins, 5-1 on aggregate.

Campbell was replaced by his assistant Ian Porterfield in May 1991 and within two months Durie also left Stamford Bridge, moving to Spurs for a club record £2.2 million.

Porterfield's side made a good start to 1991-92 and were still fifth after the first 11 games. They faded, but were then buoyed again by an eight match unbeaten start to 1992. Hopes were raised of F.A. Cup glory but these evaporated at Second Division Sunderland in a quarter-final replay. The Blues' League form suffered during the last third of the season and they limply finished in 14th place.

Kerry Dixon departed to Southampton after netting 147 League goals from 335 games in a Chelsea shirt. Only five were netted in his last season – 1991-92 – when Dennis Wise top scored (with 10).

After paying Norwich City a club record £2.3 million for Robert Fleck in the close season, Chelsea appeared to recover from a mixed start to 1992-93, by winning six out of seven matches between mid October and early December. It only proved to be a prelude to a serious slump that lasted 12 matches without a win - by which time Porterfield had been axed and replaced on a caretaker basis by David Webb.

Webb, the scorer of the winning goal in the 1970 F.A. Cup final replay, steered his old club into 11th place; but it was Glenn Hoddle who was appointed the new manager shortly after he led Swindon into the top-flight via the play-offs.

Hoddle's new side showed promising early season form and lodged in mid table before a 11 match winless run (including six defeats on the trot) spun them into relegation trouble. Three successive victories just after Christmas planted a seed of hope and they improved to finish 1993-94 in 14th place. Mark Stein top scored with 13 from just 18 games. Injury forced him to miss 12 of the last 13 League games and in the meantime his club progressed to the F.A. Cup final.

During this Cup run, two games were required to shake off both Barnet and Sheffield Wednesday – the latter were defeated 3-1 at Hillsborough. Chelsea then took the second-flight scalps of Oxford (away), Wolves (at home) and Luton (2-0 in a Wembley semi-final) to set up a final with League Champions Manchester United.

Having completed the double over the Old Trafford side in the League, the Londoners were not overawed in the Wembley final. They had the better of a goalless first half and only crumbled after Eric Cantona stuck home two penalties in seven minutes. The 4-0 scoreline was far from a true reflection of Chelsea's contribution to the match.

With United entering the Champions Cup, Hoddle's side qualified for the 1994-95 European Cup Winners' Cup. Viktoria Zizkov proved extremely dangerous opponents in the first round, scoring twice in the first half at the Bridge. Chelsea still took a 4-2 lead into the second leg and it proved just enough as Hoddle's depleted squad progressed despite losing 1-0. The second round proved even tougher with FK Austria holding the Blues to a goalless draw at Stamford Bridge. A goal by John Spencer put Hoddle's side into the driving seat in the replay; but an equaliser meant more tension before Chelsea progressed on the away goals rule.

The next opponents were FC Brugge and after limiting the Belgians to a single goal advantage in the away leg, almost 29,000 fans cheered Chelsea on to a 2-0 victory at Stamford Bridge, with Stein and Paul Furlong netting in the first half. The semi-final draw kept Chelsea and Arsenal (the holders) apart; but neither London side was to win the competition as Real Zaragoza claimed them both. The Blues' hopes seemed to have evaporated when they lost the semi-final first leg 3-0 away. However, they showed considerable spirit on their home pitch, but Aragon's goal for the Spanish Cup winners rendered the efforts by Furlong, Frank Sinclair and Stein worthless.

Chelsea made a promising start to the 1994-95 League campaign and wedged themselves in the top eight for most of the first half of the term. A poor spell of just two wins from 19 games took the wind out of their sails; but they improved again to finish 11th.

After taking five games to get their first win, Hoddle's side were always comfortably placed in mid table in 1995-96. They generally played some fine football with the Dutch master Ruud Gullit running the show. However, despite the acquisition of Mark Hughes (from Manchester United) a lack of fire-power hindered them. Spencer was the top scorer with 13 (out of 46) as Chelsea again finished 11th.

The Blues enjoyed a fine F.A. Cup run in 1995-96, but were again denied by Manchester United, this time in a Villa Park semi-final. After Gullit deservedly headed them into a first half lead, injuries to both full-backs allowed their opponents (who were again to win the double) to get into the match and win the game 2-1. Earlier, Chelsea had knocked out Newcastle in a St. James' Park replay (on penalties), QPR, Grimsby and Wimbledon.

With Hoddle departing to take charge of the national side, Gullit stepped up during the summer of 1996 to become the main man on and off the field. And with Stamford Bridge gleaming after its expensive face-lift, Chelsea look forward with great anticipation and the burning desire to capture that elusive fifth major trophy.

Stamford Bridge pictured during the 1995-96 Season.
Revelopment of the South Terrace (below) is currently underway.

F.A. CUP

1971/72 SEASON
3rd Round
Jan 15 vs Birmingham City (a) 1-0
Att: 22,135 Dempsey

4th Round
Feb 5 vs Bolton Wanderers (h) 3-0
Att: 38,066 Cooke, Houseman, Hollins (pen)

5th Round
Feb 26 vs Orient (a) 2-3
Att: 30,329 Webb, Osgood

1972/73 SEASON
3rd Round
Jan 13 vs Brighton & Hove Albion (a) 2-0
Att: 29,287 Osgood 2

4th Round
Feb 3 vs Ipswich Town (h) 2-0
Att: 36,461 Garner 2

5th Round
Feb 24 vs Sheffield Wednesday (a) 2-1
Att: 46,910 Osgood, Garner

6th Round
Mar 17 vs Arsenal (h) 2-2
Att: 37,685 Hollins, Osgood

Replay
Mar 20 vs Arsenal (a) 1-2
Att: 62,642 Houseman

1973/74 SEASON
3rd Round
Jan 5 vs Queen's Park Rangers (h) 0-0
Att: 31,540

Replay
Jan 15 vs Queen's Park Rangers (a) 0-1
Att: 28,573

1974/75 SEASON
3rd Round
Jan 4 vs Sheffield Wednesday (h) 3-2
Att: 24,679 Droy 2, Garland

4th Round
Jan 25 vs Birmingham City (h) 0-1
Att: 35,450

1975/76 SEASON
3rd Round
Jan 1 vs Bristol Rovers (h) 1-1
Att: 35,226 Garner

Replay
Jan 3 vs Bristol Rovers (a) 1-0
Att: 13,939 Swain

4th Round
Jan 24 vs York City (a) 2-0
Att: 9,591 Garner, Hutchinson

5th Round
Feb 14 vs Crystal Palace (h) 2-3
Att: 54,407 R. Wilkins, Wicks

1976/77 SEASON
3rd Round
Jan 8 vs Southampton (a) 1-1
Att: 26,041 Locke

Replay
Jan 12 vs Southampton (h) 0-3 (aet)
Att: 42,868

1977/78 SEASON
3rd Round
Jan 7 vs Liverpool (h) 4-2
Att: 45,449 Walker 2, Finniestone, Langley

4th Round
Jan 31 vs Burnley (h) 6-2
Att: 32,168 Droy, Wicks, Swain (pen), Walker, Langley, R. Wilkins

5th Round
Feb 18 vs Orient (h) 0-0
Att: 25,123

Replay
Feb 27 vs Orient (h) 1-2
Att: 36,379 Roffey (og)

1978/79 SEASON
3rd Round
Jan 15 vs Manchester United (a) 0-3
Att: 38,500

1979/80 SEASON
3rd Round
Jan 14 vs Wigan Athletic (h) 0-1
Att: 22,300

1980/81 SEASON
3rd Round
Jan 3 vs Southampton (a) 1-3
Att: 23,694 Lee

1981/82 SEASON
3rd Round
Jan 18 vs Hull City (h) 0-0
Att: 14,899

Replay
Jan 21 vs Hull City (a) 2-0
Att: 13,238 Bumstead, Mayes

4th Round
Jan 23 vs Wrexham (h) 0-0
Att: 17,226

Replay
Jan 26 vs Wrexham (a) 1-1 (aet)
Att: 8,655 Mayes

2nd Replay
Feb 1 vs Wrexham (a) 2-1
Att: 10,647 Droy, Mayes

5th Round
Feb 13 vs Liverpool (h) 2-0
Att: 41,422 Rhoades-Brown, Lee

6th Round
Mar 6 vs Tottenham Hotspur (h) 2-3
Att: 42,557 Mayes, Fillery

1982/83 SEASON
3rd Round
Jan 8 vs Huddersfield Town (a) 1-1
Att: 17,004 Mayes

Replay
Jan 12 vs Huddersfield Town (h) 2-0
Att: 14,417 Bumstead, Fillery

4th Round
Jan 29 vs Derby County (a) 1-2
Att: 23,383 Fillery

1983/84 SEASON
3rd Round
Jan 7 vs Blackburn Rovers (a) 0-1
Att: 10,940

1984/85 SEASON
3rd Round
Jan 5 vs Wigan Athletic (h) 2-2
Att: 16,220 Nevin, Speedie

Replay
Jan 26 vs Wigan Athletic (a) 5-0
Att: 9,708 Dixon 4 (1 pen), Speedie

4th Round
Feb 4 vs Millwall (h) 2-3
Att: 25,148 Spackman, Canoville

1985/86 SEASON
3rd Round
Jan 4 vs Shrewsbury Town (a) 1-0
Att: 8,100 Speedie

4th Round
Jan 26 vs Liverpool (h) 1-2
Att: 33,625 Speedie

1986/87 SEASON
3rd Round
Jan 10 vs Aston Villa (a) 2-2
Att: 21,997 Bumstead, Speedie

Replay
Jan 21 vs Aston Villa (h) 2-1
Att: 13,473 Durie, Hazard (pen)

4th Round
Feb 1 vs Watford (a) 0-1
Att: 18,832

1987/88 SEASON
3rd Round
Jan 9 vs Derby County (a) 3-1
Att: 18,753 McAllister, Dixon, Wegerle

4th Round
Jan 30 vs Manchester United (a) 0-2
Att: 50,746

1988/89 SEASON
3rd Round
Jan 7 vs Barnsley (a) 0-4
Att: 13,241

1989/90 SEASON
3rd Round
Jan 6 vs Crewe Alexandra (h) 1-1
Att: 18,066 Clarke

Replay
Jan 10 vs Crewe Alexandra (a) 2-0
Att: 7,200 Dixon 2

4th Round
Jan 27 vs Bristol City (a) 1-3
Att: 24,535 K. Wilson

1990/91 SEASON
3rd Round
Jan 5 vs Oxford United (h) 1-3
Att: 14,586 Dixon

1991/92 SEASON
3rd Round
Jan 4 vs Hull City (a) 2-0
Att: 13,580 Jones, Wise

4th Round
Jan 26 vs Everton (h) 1-0
Att: 21,132 Allen

5th Round
Feb 15 vs Sheffield United (h) 1-0
Att: 34,447 Stuart

6th Round
Mar 9 vs Sunderland (h) 1-1
Att: 33,948 Allen

Replay
Mar 18 vs Sunderland (a) 1-2
Att: 26,039 Wise

1992/93 SEASON
3rd Round
Jan 13 vs Middlesbrough (a) 1-2
Att: 10,776 Mohan (og)

1993/94 SEASON
3rd Round
Jan 8 vs Barnet (at Stamford Bridge) 0-0
Att: 23,200

Replay
Jan 19 vs Barnet (h) 4-0
Att: 16,209 Burley, Peacock, Stein, Shipperley

4th Round
Jan 29 vs Sheffield Wednesday (h) 1-1
Att: 26,094 Peacock

Replay
Feb 9 vs Sheffield Wednesday (a) 3-1 (aet)
Att: 26,144 Spencer, Peacock, Burley

5th Round
Feb 19 vs Oxford United (a) 2-1
Att: 10,787 Spencer, Burley

6th Round
Mar 13 vs Wolverhampton Wands. (h) 1-0
Att: 29,340 Peacock

Semi-Final (at Wembley)
Apr 9 vs Luton Town 2-0
Att: 59,989 Peacock 2

FINAL (at Wembley)
May 14 vs Manchester United 0-4
Att: 79,634

1994/95 SEASON
3rd Round
Jan 7 vs Charlton Athletic (h) 3-0
Att: 24,485 Peacock, Sinclair, Spencer
4th Round
Jan 28 vs Millwall (a) 0-0
Att: 18,573
Replay
Feb 8 vs Millwall (h) 1-1 (aet)
Att: 25,515 Stein
Millwall won 5-4 on penalties

1995/96 SEASON
3rd Round
Jan 7 vs Newcastle United (h) 1-1
Att: 25,151 Hughes
Replay
Jan 17 vs Newcastle United (a) 2-2 (aet)
Att: 36,535 Wise (pen), Gullit
Chelsea won 4-2 on penalties
4th Round
Jan 29 vs Queen's Park Rangers (a) 2-1
Att: 18,542 Peacock, Furlong
5th Round
Feb 21 vs Grimsby Town (a) 0-0
Att: 9,448
Replay
Feb 28 vs Grimsby Town (h) 4-1
Att: 28,545 Duberry, Hughes, Spencer, Peacock
6th Round
Mar 9 vs Wimbledon (h) 2-2
Att: 30,805 Hughes, Gullit
Replay
Mar 20 vs Wimbledon (a) 3-1
Att: 21,380 Petrescu, Duberry, Hughes
Semi-Final (at Villa Park)
Mar 31 vs Manchester United 1-2
Att: 38,421 Gullit

LEAGUE CUP
1971/72 SEASON
2nd Round
Sep 8 vs Plymouth Argyle (h) 2-0
Att: 23,011 Houseman, Hollins
3rd Round
Oct 6 vs Nottingham Forest (a) 1-1
Att: 16,811 Webb
Replay
Oct 11 vs Nottingham Forest (h) 2-1
Att: 24,817 Baldwin, Osgood
4th Round
Oct 27 vs Bolton Wanderers (h) 1-1
Att: 27,679 Hudson
Replay
Nov 8 vs Bolton Wanderers (a) 6-0
Att: 29,805 Cooke, Baldwin 3, Hollins 2 (1 pen)
5th Round
Nov 17 vs Norwich City (a) 1-0
Att: 35,927 Osgood
Semi-Final (1st leg)
Dec 22 vs Tottenham Hotspur (h) 3-2
Att: 43,330 Osgood, Garland, Hollins (pen)
Semi-Final (2nd leg)
Jan 5 vs Tottenham Hotspur (a) 2-2 (agg 5-4)
Att: 52,755 Garland, Hudson

FINAL (at Wembley)
Mar 4 vs Stoke City (h) 1-2
Att: 100,000 Osgood

1972/73 SEASON
2nd Round
Sep 6 vs Southend United (a) 1-0
Att: 24,160 Garland
3rd Round
Oct 4 vs Derby County (a) 0-0
Att: 28,065
Replay
Oct 9 vs Derby County (h) 3-2
Att: 26,395 Kember, Webb, Osgood
4th Round
Oct 31 vs Bury (a) 1-0
Att: 16,226 Garland
5th Round
Nov 22 vs Notts County (h) 3-1
Att: 22,580 Osgood, Garland, Kember
Semi-Final (1st leg)
Dec 13 vs Norwich City (h) 0-2
Att: 34,316
Semi-Final (2nd leg)
Jan 3 vs Norwich City (a) 0-1 (aggreg. 0-3)
Att: 34,265

1973/74 SEASON
2nd Round
Oct 8 vs Stoke City (a) 0-1
Att: 17,281

1974/75 SEASON
2nd Round
Sep 11 vs Newport County (h) 4-2
Att: 13,322 Cooke, Garland 3
3rd Round
Oct 9 vs Stoke City (h) 2-2
Att: 19,954 Hutchison 2
Replay
Oct 16 vs Stoke City (a) 1-1
Att: 24,377 Britton
2nd Replay
Oct 22 vs Stoke City (a) 2-6
Att: 26,712 Hollins, Baldwin

1975/76 SEASON
2nd Round
Sep 9 vs Crewe Alexandra (a) 0-1
Att: 6,723

1976/77 SEASON
2nd Round
Sep 1 vs Sheffield United (h) 3-1
Att: 16,883 Wilkins R. 2, Swain
3rd Round
Sep 20 vs Huddersfield Town (h) 2-0
Att: 19,860 Finnieston 2
4th Round
Oct 26 vs Arsenal (h) 1-2
Att: 52,305 Hay

1977/78 SEASON
2nd Round
Aug 30 vs Liverpool (a) 0-2
Att: 33,170

1978/79 SEASON
2nd Round
Aug 29 vs Bolton Wanderers (h) 1-2
Att: 10,748 Langley

1979/80 SEASON
2nd Round (1st leg)
Aug 28 vs Plymouth Argyle (a) 2-2
Att: 10,802 Fillery 2
2nd Round (2nd leg)
Sep 4 vs Plymouth Argyle (h) 1-2 (agg. 3-4)
Att: 14,112 Droy

1980/81 SEASON
3rd Round
Jan 3 vs Southampton (a) 1-3
Att: 23,694 Lee

1981/82 SEASON
3rd Round
Jan 18 vs Hull City (h) 0-0
Att: 14,899
Replay
Jan 21 vs Hull City (a) 2-0
Att: 13,238 Mayes, Bumstead
4th Round
Jan 23 vs Wrexham (h) 0-0
Att: 17,226
Replay
Jan 26 vs Wrexham (a) 1-1
Att: 8,655 Mayes
2nd Replay
Feb 1 vs Wrexham (a) 2-1
Att: 10,647 Droy, Mayes
5th Round
Feb 13 vs Liverpool (h) 2-0
Att: 41,422 Rhoades-Brown, Lee
6th Round
Mar 6 vs Tottenham Hotspur (h) 2-3
Att: 42,557 Fillery, Mayes

1982/83 SEASON
3rd Round
Jan 8 vs Huddersfield Town (a) 1-1
Att: 17,004 Mayes
Replay
Jan 12 vs Huddersfield Town (h) 2-0
Att: 14,417 Bumstead, Fillery
4th Round
Jan 29 vs Derby County (a) 1-2
Att: 23,383 Fillery

1983/84 SEASON
3rd Round
Nov 9 vs West Bromwich Albion (h) 0-1
Att: 22,932

1984/85 SEASON
3rd Round
Oct 30 vs Walsall (a) 2-2
Att: 11,102 Nevin, Lee
Replay
Nov 6 vs Walsall (h) 3-0
Att: 19,502 Speedie, Dixon, Jones K.
4th Round
Nov 21 vs Manchester City (h) 4-1
Att: 26,364 Dixon 3, Jones K.
Quarter-Final
Jan 28 vs Sheffield Wednesday (h) 1-1
Att: 36,028 Speedie
Replay
Jan 30 vs Sheffield Wednesday (a) 4-4 (aet)
Att: 36,509 Canoville 2, Dixon, Thomas
2nd Replay
Feb 6 vs Sheffield Wednesday (h) 2-1
Att: 36,395 Speedie, Thomas
Semi-Final (1st leg)
Feb 13 vs Sunderland (a) 0-2
Att: 32,440
Semi-Final (2nd leg)
Mar 4 vs Sunderland (h) 2-3 (aggregate 2-5)
Att: 38,440 Speedie, Nevin

1985/86 SEASON
3rd Round
Oct 29 vs Fulham (h) 1-1
Att: 19,669 Hazard
Replay
Nov 6 vs Fulham (a) 1-0
Att: 20,190 Dixon

4th Round
Nov 26 vs Everton (h) 2-2
Att: 27,544 Dixon, Nevin
Replay
Dec 10 vs Everton (a) 2-1
Att: 26,376 Dixon, McLaughlin
Quarter-Final
Jan 22 vs Queen's Park Rangers (a) 1-1
Att: 27,000 Byrne
Replay
Jan 29 vs Queen's Park Rangers (h) 0-2
Att: 27,937

1986/87 SEASON
3rd Round
Oct 28 vs Cardiff City (a) 1-2
Att: 8,018 Jones (pen)

1987/88 SEASON
2nd Round (1st leg)
Sep 23 vs Reading (a) 1-3
Att: 11,034 Durie (pen)
2nd Round (2nd leg)
Oct 7 vs Reading (h) 3-2 (aggregate 4-5)
Att: 15,469 Durie 3 (1 pen)

1988/89 SEASON
2nd Round (1st leg)
Sep 27 vs Scunthorpe United (a) 1-4
Att: 5,061 Lister (og)
2nd Round (2nd leg)
Oct 12 vs Scunthorpe Utd. (h) 2-2 (agg. 3-6)
Att: 5,814 Wilson K, Dixon

1989/90 SEASON
2nd Round (1st leg)
Sep 19 vs Scarborough (h) 1-1
Att: 10,349 Roberts
2nd Round (2nd leg)
Oct 4 vs Scarborough (a) 2-3 (aggreg. 3-4)
Att: 5,086 Clarke, Wilson K.

1990/91 SEASON
2nd Round (1st leg)
Sep 26 vs Walsall (a) 5-0
Att: 5,666 Townsend 2, Wilson, McAlister, Dixon
2nd Round (2nd leg)
Oct 10 vs Walsall (h) 4-1 (aggregate 9-1)
Att: 10,037 Durie, Dixon 2, Le Saux
3rd Round
Oct 31 vs Portsmouth (h) 0-0
Att: 16,699
Replay
Nov 6 vs Portsmouth (a) 3-2
Att: 16,085 Lee, Wise (pen), Wilson
4th Round
Nov 28 vs Oxford United (a) 2-1
Att: 9,789 Durie 2
5th Round
Jan 16 vs Tottenham Hotspur (h) 0-0
Att: 34,178
Replay
Jan 23 vs Tottenham Hotspur (a) 3-0
Att: 33,861 Townsend, Dixon, Wise (pen)
Semi-Final (1st leg)
Feb 24 vs Sheffield Wednesday (h) 0-2
Att: 34,014
Semi-Final (2nd leg)
Feb 27 vs Sheffield Wed. (a) 1-3 (agg. 1-5)
Att: 34,669 Stuart

1991/92 SEASON
2nd Round (1st leg)
Sep 25 vs Tranmere Rovers (h) 1-1
Att: 11,311 Townsend
2nd Round (2nd leg)
Oct 8 vs Tranmere Rovers (a) 1-3 (agg 2-4)
Att: 11,165 Wise

1992/93 SEASON
2nd Round (1st leg)
Sep 23 vs Walsall (h) 3-0
Att: 5,510 Wise, Newton, Townsend
2nd Round (2nd leg)
Oct 7 vs Walsall (a) 1-0 (aggregate 4-0)
Att: 7,646 Fleck (pen)
3rd Round
Oct 28 vs Newcastle United (h) 2-1
Att: 30,193 Sinclair, Harford
4th Round
Dec 2 vs Everton (a) 2-2
Att: 14,457 Harford, Stuart
Replay
Dec 16 vs Everton (h) 1-0
Att: 19,496 Townsend
5th Round
Jan 6 vs Crystal Palace (a) 1-3
Att: 28,510 Townsend

1993/94 SEASON
2nd Round (1st leg)
Sep 22 vs West Bromwich Albion (a) 1-1
Att: 14,919 Shipperley
2nd Round (2nd leg)
Oct 6 vs West Bromwich A (h) 2-1 (agg 3-2)
Att: 11,959 Wise 2
3rd Round
Oct 26 vs Manchester City (a) 0-1
Att: 16,713

1994/95 SEASON
2nd Round (1st leg)
Sep 21 vs Bournemouth (h) 1-0
Att: 8,974 Rocastle
2nd Round (2nd leg)
Oct 4 vs Bournemouth (a) 1-0 (aggreg. 2-0)
Att: 9,784 Peacock
3rd Round
Oct 26 vs West Ham United (a) 0-1
Att: 18,815

1995/96 SEASON
2nd Round (1st leg)
Sep 20 vs Stoke City (a) 0-0
Att: 15,574
2nd Round (2nd leg)
Oct 4 vs Stoke City (h) 0-1 (aggregate 0-1)
Att: 16,272

EUROPEAN CUP WINNERS CUP
1971/72 SEASON
1st Round (1st leg)
Sep 15 vs Jeunesse Hautcharge (a) 8-0
Att: 13,000 Osgood 3, Houseman 2, Hollins, Webb, Baldwin
1st Round (2nd leg)
Sep 29 vs Jeunesse Haut. (h) 13-0 (agg 21-0)
Att: 27,621 Osgood 5, Baldwin 3, Hollins (pen), Hudson, Webb, Houseman, Harris
2nd Round (1st leg)
Oct 20 vs Atvidaberg (a) 0-0
Att: 10,212
2nd Round (2nd leg)
Nov 3 vs Atvidaberg (h) 1-1 (aet) (agg. 1-1)
Att: 28,071 Hudson
Atvidaberg won on the Away Goals rule

1994/95 SEASON
1st Round (1st leg)
Sep 15 vs Viktoria Zizkov (h) 4-2
Att: 22,036 Furlong, Sinclair, Rocastle, Wise
1st Round (2nd leg)
Sep 29 vs Viktoria Zizkov (a) 0-0 (agg. 4-2)
Att: 6,000

2nd Round (1st leg)
Oct 20 vs FK Austria (h) 0-0
Att: 22,560
2nd Round (2nd leg)
Nov 3 vs FK Austria (a) 1-1 (aet) (agg. 1-1)
Att: 25,000 Spencer
Chelsea won on the Away Goals rule
Quarter-Final (1st leg)
Feb 28 vs FC Brugge (a) 0-1
Att: 18,000
Quarter-Final (2nd leg)
Mar 14 vs FC Brugge (h) 2-0 (aggreg. 2-1)
Att: 28,661 Stein, Furlong
Semi-Final (1st leg)
Apr 6 vs Zaragoza (a) 0-3
Att: 35,000
Semi-Final (2nd leg)
Apr 20 vs Zaragoza (h) 3-1 (aggregate 3-4)
Att: 35,000 Furlong, Sinclair, Stein

1971-72

1	Aug	(a)	14	Arsenal	L	0-3		49,174
2		(h)	18	Manchester U	L	2-3	Baldwin, Osgood	54,763
3		(h)	21	Manchester C	D	2-2	Baldwin, Weller	38,425
4		(a)	24	Everton	L	0-2		38,994
5		(a)	28	Huddersfield T	W	2-1	Hollins (pen), Osgood	15,030
6	Sep	(h)	1	West Brom A	W	1-0	Hollins	29,931
7		(h)	4	Coventry C	D	3-3	Osgood 2, Hollins	35,459
8		(a)	11	West Ham U	L	1-2	Hollins	36,866
9		(h)	18	Derby Co	D	1-1	Baldwin	42,872
10		(a)	25	Sheffield U	L	0-1		40,651
11	Oct	(h)	2	Wolverhampton W	W	3-1	Baldwin, Houseman, Hollins	42,706
12		(a)	9	Liverpool	D	0-0		48,464
13		(h)	16	Arsenal	L	1-2	Osgood	52,338
14		(h)	23	Southampton	W	3-0	Baldwin, Kember, Hollins (pen)	38,940
15		(a)	30	Leicester C	D	1-1	Osgood	36,574
16	Nov	(h)	6	Nottingham F	W	2-0	Cooke, Osgood	25,812
17		(a)	13	Stoke C	W	1-0	Osgood	22,190
18		(a)	20	Crystal Palace	W	3-2	Baldwin, Hudson, Osgood	34,637
19		(h)	27	Tottenham H	W	1-0	Cooke	52,581
20	Dec	(a)	4	Newcastle U	D	0-0		38,562
21		(h)	11	Leeds U	D	0-0		45,867
22		(a)	18	Coventry C	D	1-1	Osgood	22,424
23		(h)	27	Ipswich T	W	2-0	Kember, Garland	43,896
24	Jan	(a)	1	Derby Co	L	0-1		33,633
25		(h)	8	Huddersfield T	D	2-2	Hollins, Osgood	30,801
26		(a)	22	Manchester U	W	1-0	Osgood	55,927
27		(h)	29	Everton	W	4-0	Osgood 2, Hollins (pen), Dempsey	38,558
28	Feb	(h)	19	Leicester C	W	2-1	Osgood 2	37,783
29	Mar	(h)	11	Liverpool	D	0-0		38,691
30		(a)	14	Nottingham F	L	1-2	Hollins (pen)	13,346
31		(a)	18	Manchester C	L	0-1		53,322
32		(h)	25	West Ham	W	3-1	Osgood, Mulligan, Hollins	45,137
33		(h)	29	Sheffield U	W	2-0	Webb 2	28,444
34	Apr	(a)	1	Ipswich T	W	2-1	Webb 2	24,325
35		(h)	8	Crystal Palace	W	2-1	Hollins, Osgood	34,105
36		(a)	12	Wolverhampton W	W	2-0	Garland, Osgood	24,566
37		(a)	15	Tottenham H	L	0-3		45,799
38		(a)	18	Southampton	D	2-2	Baldwin 2	24,933
39		(h)	22	Newcastle U	D	3-3	Baldwin 2, Kember	33,000
40		(h)	24	Stoke C	W	2-0	Hudson, Garland	23,443
41		(a)	27	West Brom A	L	0-4		18,489
42	May	(a)	1	Leeds U	L	0-2		46,565

FINAL LEAGUE POSITION: 7th in Division One

Appearances

Sub. Appearances

Goals

16

Bonetti P	McCreadie E	Harris R	Hollins J	Dempsey J	Webb D	Smethurst D	Hudson A	Osgood P	Baldwin T	Houseman P	Phillips J	Boyle J	Cooke C	Weller K	Mulligan P	Garland C	Hinton M	Kember S	Sherwood S	Feely P	Potrac A	Droy M	
1	2	3	4	5	6	7	8	9	10	11													1
	2	6	4	5		7	8	9	10	11*	1	3	12										2
		2	3	4	5	6		9	10		1	8	11	7									3
		2*	3	4	5	6		9	10	12	1	8	11	7									4
		3	4	5	6		8	9		10	1	11	7		2								5
		3	4	5	6		8	9		10	1	11	7		2								6
.		3	4	5	6			9		11	1	10	7		2	8							7
		3	4	5	6		8	9		11	1		7		2	10							8
1		3	4		5		10	9	8	11		2	7			6							9
1		3	4		5		10	9	7	11		2				6		8					10
1		3	4		5		10	9	8	11		2	7			6							11
1		3	4		5			9	8	11		2	7			6		10					12
1		3	4		5	7		9	8			2	11			6		10					13
1		3	4	5	6		10	9	7				11		2			8					14
1		3	8	5	6		10	9				4	11		2			7					15
1		3	4	5	6		10	9		11		2	7					8					16
1		3	4	5	6		10	9	8	11		2	7										17
1		3	4	5	6		10	9	8*	11		2	7					12					18
1		3	4	5	6		10	9		11			7		2			8					19
1		3	4	5	6		10	9		11			7		2			8					20
1		3	4	5	6		10	9		11			7		2			8					21
1*		3	4	5	6		10	9		11			7		2	12		8					22
	2	4	5	1			10	9		11*		3	12		6	7		8					23
		3	4	5	6		10	9		11			12		2	7		8*	1				24
1	2	3	10	5	6*			9		11			4					8		12	7		25
1		3	4	5	6		10	9					7		2	11		8					26
1		3	4	5	6		10	9					7		2	11		8					27
1	3	6	4		5		10	9		11			7		2			8					28
1	2	4	5		6		10	9	11	3			7		8								29
1	2	4	5		6			9*	11	3			7		8	12		10					30
1		4	5		6		10	9	11*	3			7		2	8		12					31
1	6	4	5		8		10	9	3				11		2			7					32
1	6	4	5		8		10	9	3				11		2			7					33
1	6	4	5		8		10	9	3				11		2			7					34
1	6	4	5		8		10	9	3				11		2	7							35
1	6	4	5		8		10	9	3				11		2	7							36
1	6	4	5		8		10	9*	3				11		2	7		12					37
1		3	4	5	6		10	9					11		2	7		8					38
1		3	4	5	6		10	9					11		2	7		8					39
1		3	4		6		10	9					11		2	7		8		5			40
1		3	4	5	6		10	9	11				7		2			8					41
1	3	2	4	5	6		10	9	11				7					8					42
33	7	41	42	35	41	2	36	36	20	26	7	24	35	2	27	16	5	24	1		1	1	
										1			3			1	1	3		1			
		11	1	4		2	19	10	1		2	1	1	3		3							

17

1972-73

1	Aug	12	(h)	Leeds U	W	4-0	Osgood. Cooke, Garland 2	51,102
2		16	(a)	Leicester C	D	1-1	Garland	22,873
3		19	(a)	Derby Co	W	2-1	Harris, Garland	31,868
4		23	(h)	Liverpool	L	1-2	Garland	35,375
5		26	(h)	Manchester C	W	2-1	Osgood, Houseman	30,845
6		30	(a)	Manchester U	D	0-0		44,482
7	Sep	2	(a)	Arsenal	D	1-1	Cooke	46,675
8		9	(h)	West Ham U	L	1-3	Garland	34,392
9		16	(a)	Sheffield U	L	1-2	Garland	24,458
10		23	(h)	Ipswich T	W	2-0	Osgood, Feely	29,647
11		30	(a)	Coventry C	W	3-1	Garner, Blockley (og), Houseman	20,058
12	Oct	7	(a)	Birmingham C	D	2-2	Osgood, Webb	38,756
13		14	(h)	West Brom A	W	3-1	Osgood, Garland, Webb	28,998
14		21	(a)	Tottenham H	W	1-0	Hollins	47,429
15		28	(h)	Newcastle U	D	1-1	McCreadie	35,273
16	Nov	4	(a)	Liverpool	L	1-3	Baldwin	48,932
17		11	(h)	Leicester C	D	1-1	Garner	28,456
18		18	(a)	Southampton	L	1-3	Osgood	24,164
19		25	(h)	Crystal Palace	D	0-0		36,608
20	Dec	2	(a)	Stoke C	D	1-1	Osgood	21,274
21		9	(h)	Norwich C	W	1-1	Garner, Hutchinson 2	29,998
22		16	(a)	Wolverhampton W	L	0-1		20,799
23		23	(h)	Everton	D	1-1	Hutchinson	23,385
24		26	(a)	Ipswich T	L	0-3		26,243
25		30	(h)	Derby Co	D	1-1	Osgood	29,794
26	Jan	20	(h)	Arsenal	L	0-1		36,292
27		27	(a)	West Ham U	L	1-3	Garner	33,336
28	Feb	10	(h)	Sheffield U	W	4-2	Garland 2, Garner 2	21,464
29		17	(a)	Leeds U	D	1-1	Osgood	41,781
30	Mar	3	(h)	Birmingham C	D	0-0		26,259
31		6	(h)	Wolverhampton W	L	0-2		18,868
32		10	(a)	West Brom A	D	1-1	Garland	21,820
33		24	(a)	Newcastle U	D	1-1	Howard (og)	21,729
34		27	(a)	Manchester C	W	1-0	Osgood	23,973
35		31	(a)	Crystal Palace	L	0-2		39,325
36	Apr	3	(h)	Tottenham H	L	0-1		25,536
37		7	(h)	Stoke C	L	1-3	Ord	19,706
38		14	(a)	Norwich C	L	0-1		24,753
39		18	(a)	Everton	L	0-1		24,999
40		21	(h)	Southampton	W	2-1	Brolly, Hollins	19,699
41		23	(h)	Coventry C	W	2-0	Hinton, Hollins (pen)	18,279
42		28	(h)	Manchester U	W	1-0	Osgood	44,184

FINAL LEAGUE POSITION: 12th in Division One

Appearances

Sub. Appearances

Goals

Bonetti P	Harris R	McCreadie E	Hollins J	Dempsey J	Webb D	Garland C	Kember S	Osgood P	Hudson A	Cooke C	Droy M	Phillips J	Houseman P	Mulligan P	Garner W	Boyle J	Bason B	Feely P	Locke G	Hinton M	Sherwood S	Baldwin T	Hutchinson I	Brolly M	Britton I	Ord T	Match
1	2	3	4	5	6	7	8	9	10	11																	1
1	2	3	4	5	6	7	8	9	10	11																	2
1	2	3	4		6	7	8	9	10	11	5																3
	2	3	4		6	7	8	9	10	11	5*	1	12														4
1	6	3	4		5	7	8	9	10	11*			12	2													5
1	6	3*	4		5	7	8	9	10	12			11	2													6
1	6	3	4		5	7	8*	9		11	12		10	2													7
1	6	3	4		5	7	8	9	10*				11	2	12												8
1	4	3	10		6*	11	8			5			2		12	7	9										9
1	6	3	4			7	8	9		11	5		2		10												10
1	6	3	4		5	7	8	9					11		10*		2	12									11
1	6	3	4	10		7	8	9			5		11				2										12
1	6	3	4	10		7	8	9			5		11				2										13
1	6	3	4		5	10	8	9					11			7	2										14
1	6	3	4		5		8	9					11		10	7	2										15
	6	3	4		5	10	8						11		9		2		1	7							16
	6	3	4		5	7	8	9					11		10		2		1								17
	6	3	4		5		8	9	10				11		7		2		1								18
	2	3	4		6		8	9	10		5	1	11		7												19
	2	3	4		6		8	9	10		5	1	11		7												20
	2	3	4		6			9	8		5	1	11		7								10				21
	6		4		5	7	10*	9	8			1	3		11		2	12									22
		3	4	5	6	11	8					1	10*		12		2					7	9				23
	2		4	5	6	11		9	8			1	10*		12							7					24
		3	4	5	2			9	8			1	10						6			7	11*	12			25
		3	4	5	6	10		9	8			1	11				2					7					26
		3	4	5	6		8	9	10			1	11				2					7					27
	6		4	5*		11	10	9	8			1	3		7	12	2										28
		3	4		7	6	9	8				1	11		10		2		5								29
		3	4		11	6	9	8				1			10		2		5						7		30
		3	4		7	6	9	8				1			10		2		5						11		31
		3	4		9	8	6	7				1			10		2		5						11		32
	6	3	2			10	4		8			1	11*		9				12	5					7		33
1	6	3	2			7	4	9	8				10							5					11		34
1	6	3	2	12			4	9	8				10*		7					5					11		35
1	2	3	4	5		10	7*	9	8										6					12	11		36
1	2	3	4	5				9								8			6					11	7	10	37
1	2	3	4					9							10	8			6	5				11	7		38
1	2	3	4					9							10*	8			6	5				11	12	7	39
1	2	3	4					10							9	8			6	5				11	12	7*	40
1	2	3	4					10							9*	8		12	6	5				11	7		41
1	2	3	4					10							9	8			6	5				11	7		42
23	42	31	42	10	26	27	35	38	26	7	14	16	19	6	19	5	4	2	17	15	3	11	3	6	11	3	
				1						1	1		2		2		3		1	3				1	3	1	
	1	1	3		2	11	11		2				2		6				1			1		1	3	1	

1973-74

1	Aug	25	(a)	Derby Co	L	0-1		30,666
2		28	(a)	Burnley	L	0-1		23,818
3	Sep	1	(h)	Sheffield U	L	1-2	Hollins (pen)	27,972
4		5	(h)	Birmingham C	W	3-1	Hutchinson, Hollins, Kember	25,660
5		8	(a)	Liverpool	L	0-1		47,616
6		11	(a)	Birmingham C	W	4-2	Hudson, Osgood, Baldwin 2	30,252
7		15	(h)	Coventry C	W	1-0	Osgood	30,593
8		22	(a)	Manchester C	L	2-3	Baldwin 2	32,118
9		29	(h)	Wolverhampton W	D	2-2	Garner, Osgood	27,846
10	Oct	6	(a)	Q.P.R.	D	1-1	Mancini (og)	31,009
11		13	(h)	Ipswich T	L	2-3	Baldwin, Hollins	25,111
12		20	(a)	Newcastle U	L	0-2		32,154
13		26	(h)	Norwich C	W	3-0	Baldwin 2, Kember	21,953
14	Nov	3	(a)	Manchester U	D	2-2	Baldwin, Osgood	48,036
15		10	(h)	Everton	W	3-1	Baldwin, Osgood 2	26,398
16		17	(a)	Arsenal	D	0-0		38,677
17		24	(h)	Southampton	W	4-0	Britton, Garland, Kember 2	22,596
18	Dec	8	(h)	Leicester C	W	3-2	Hollins (2 pen), Osgood	20,686
19		15	(h)	Leeds U	L	1-2	Osgood	40,768
20		22	(a)	Wolverhampton W	L	0-2		20,837
21		26	(h)	West Ham U	L	2-4	Britton, Hudson	26,982
22		29	(h)	Liverpool	L	0-1		32,901
23	Jan	1	(a)	Sheffield U	W	2-1	Kember, Hollins	32,575
24		12	(a)	Coventry C	D	2-2	Harris, Garland	20,813
25		19	(h)	Derby Co	D	1-1	Garner	27,185
26		27	(a)	Stoke C	L	0-1		31,985
27	Feb	2	(a)	Leeds U	D	1-1	Garner	41,510
28		9	(h)	Manchester C	W	1-0	Webb	20,206
29		23	(h)	Q.P.R.	D	3-3	Cooke, Garner 2	34,264
30		26	(a)	Ipswich T	D	1-1	Garland	22,415
31	Mar	2	(a)	West Ham U	L	0-3		34,043
32		9	(a)	Norwich C	D	2-2	Houseman, Kember	19,866
33		13	(h)	Burnley	W	3-0	Kember, Houseman, Hutchinson	8,171
34		16	(h)	Newcastle U	W	1-0	Hutchinson	24,207
35		23	(a)	Everton	D	1-1	Garner	29,542
36		30	(h)	Manchester U	L	1-3	Garner	29,602
37	Apr	3	(a)	Tottenham H	W	2-1	Droy, Harris	23,646
38		6	(a)	Southampton	D	0-0		27,268
39		13	(h)	Arsenal	L	1-3	Swain	29,152
40		15	(h)	Tottenham H	D	0-0		26,258
41		20	(a)	Leicester C	L	0-3		22,828
42		27	(h)	Stoke C	L	0-1		17,150

FINAL LEAGUE POSITION: 17th in Division One

Appearances

Sub. Appearances

Goals

Bonetti P	Hollins J	McCreadie E	Boyle J	Webb D	Harris R	Garland C	Kember S	Osgood P	Hutchinson I	Houseman P	Hudson A	Garner W	Droy M	Locke G	Baldwin T	Britton I	Phillips J	Wilkins G	Wilkins R	Hinton M	Brolly M	Cooke C	Sparrow J	Swain K	No.
1	2	3	4	5	6	7	8	9	10	11															1
1	2	3		5	6	7	4	9		11	8	10													2
1	2	3		5	6		4	9	10*	11	8	7	12												3
1	4			6	3	11	7	9	10		8		5	2											4
1	4			6	3		7	9	10		8	11	5	2											5
1	4	12		6	3		7*	9			8	11	5	2	10										6
1	4			6	3		7	9			8	11	5	2	10										7
1	4			6	3		7	9			8	11	5	2	10										8
1	4			6	3		7	9	12		8	11	5	2	10*										9
1	4			6	3		10	9			8	11	5	2	7										10
1	4	12		6	3		9	10		11			5	2*	8	7									11
	2	3		5	6	11	4	9		10	8				7		1								12
1	2		5*	6	7		4	9		11	8				10			3	12						13
1	4		5		7*	6		9		11	8		2		10			3	12						14
1	6			5			8	9		11	10		2	7	4							3			15
1	3			5	6	7	4	9		11			2	10	8										16
1	4			5	3	11	6	9			10		2	8	7										17
	4			5	3	11	6	9			10		2	8	7		1								18
1	4			5	3	7	6	9		11	10		2	8											19
1	4			5	6		11	9		3	10		2	8	7										20
1	4			5	3		6	9		11	10		2	8	7										21
1	4			6	3			9		11	10		5	2	8	7									22
	4			6	3	7	10			11		9*	5	2	12	8	1								23
	4			6	3	10	8						5	2	9	7	1			11					24
	4			6	3	8	9					10	5	2		7	1					11			25
	4			6	3	8	9					10	5	2		7	1					11			26
	4			6	3	8	9					10	5	2		7	1					11			27
	4			6	3	8	9					10	5	2		7	1					11			28
	4			6	3	8	9					10	5	2		7	1					11			29
	4			5	3	8	9					10	5	2		7	1					11			30
	4			6	3	8	9					10	5	2		7	1					11			31
	4			6	3	9	8	11				10	5	2			1					7			32
	4			6		8	9	12		11		10*	5	2			1					7	3		33
	4			6	3	7*	9	10	8				5	2			1					11		12	34
	4			6		9		10	8	11			5	2			1					7	3		35
	4			6	3	9		10*	8	11			5	2			1					7		12	36
	4		2					9		10			5				1	8	6			11	3	7	37
	4		2					12		9		10*	5				1	8	6			11	3	7	38
	4		2					12		9		10	5				1	8	6			11*	3	7	39
	4			6	2	8	9	10		11			5				1					7	3		40
	4			6		8	9	10*		11			5				1	2				7	3	12	41
	4			6		7		9		11			5				1	2	8				3	10	42
20	42	4	1	39	36	26	37	21	10	25	19	23	29	31	18	17	22	4	4	4	1	17	8	4	
	2							4					1		1			2					3		
	6			1	2	2	7	8	3	2	2	7	1		9	2						1		1	

21

1974-75

1	Aug	17	(h)	Carlisle U	L	0-2		31,268
2		21	(h)	Burnley	D	3-3	Houseman, Garner, Cooke	23,745
3		24	(a)	Coventry C	W	3-1	Cooke, Garner, Locke	21,251
4		27	(a)	Burnley	W	2-1	Garner, Hutchinson	17,154
5		31	(h)	Liverpool	L	0-3		39,461
6	Sept	7	(a)	Middlesbrough	D	1-1	Hutchinson	25,480
7		14	(h)	Arsenal	D	0-0		34,596
8		21	(a)	Ipswich T	L	0-2		23,121
9		25	(a)	Derby Co	L	1-4	Hutchinson	22,036
10		28	(h)	Wolverhampton W	L	0-1		23,073
11	Oct	5	(a)	Manchester C	D	1-1	Hutchinson	32,412
12		12	(h)	Tottenham H	W	1-0	Hoolins (pen)	32,660
13		19	(a)	Everton	D	1-1	Cooke	35,806
14		26	(h)	Stoke C	D	3-3	Droy, Garland, Cooke	24,718
15	Nov	2	(a)	Birmingham C	L	0-2		30,364
16		9	(h)	Leicester C	D	0-0		23,915
17		13	(h)	Coventry C .	D	3-3	Garner, Garland, Cooke	11,048
18		16	(a)	Newcastle U	L	0-5		33,821
19		30	(a)	Leeds U	L	0-2		30,444
20	Dec	7	(h)	Luton T	W	2-0	Hutchinson, Kember	19,009
21		14	(a)	Carlisle U	W	2-1	Hollins 2	12,854
22		21	(h)	West Ham U	D	1-1	Hutchinson	34,969
23		26	(a)	Arsenal	W	2-1	Garland 2	33,784
24		28	(h)	Q.P.R.	L	0-3		38,917
25	Jan	11	(a)	Luton T	D	1-1	Kember	23,096
26		18	(h)	Leeds U	L	0-2		34,733
27	Feb	1	(a)	Leicester C	D	1-1	Kember	23,759
28		8	(h)	Birmingham C	W	2-1	Wilkins R., Langley	18,144
29		15	(a)	Sheffield U	L	1-2	Garner	20,542
30		22	(h)	Newcastle U	W	3-2	Finnieston, Cooke, Hollins (pen)	26,770
31	Mar	1	(a)	Liverpool	D	2-2	Britton, Finnieston	42,762
32		8	(h)	Derby Co	L	1-2	Hollins	22,644
33		15	(a)	Wolverhampton W	L	1-7	Garner	21,649
34		18	(a)	Q.P.R.	L	0-1		25,324
35		22	(h)	Middlesbrough	L	1-2	Sparrow	22,240
36		29	(a)	West Ham U	W	1-0	Droy	31,025
37		31	(h)	Ipswich T	D	0-0		35,005
38	Apr	5	(a)	Stoke C	L	0-3		26,375
39		12	(h)	Manchester C	L	0-1		26,249
40		19	(a)	Tottenham H	L	0-2		51,064
41		23	(h)	Sheffield U	D	1-1	Maybank	23,380
42		26	(h)	Everton	D	1-1	Wilkins R.	28,432

FINAL LEAGUE POSITION: 21st in Division One

Appearances

Sub. Appearances

Goals

Bonnetti P	Locke G	Houseman P	Hollins J	Droy M	Harris R	Kember S	Hay D	Garland C	Garner W	Sissons J	Cooke C	Phillps J	Hutchinson I	Dempsey J	Wilkins R	Baldwin T	Britton I	Hinton M	Langley T	Wilkins G	Sparrow J	Finnieston S	Wicks S	Maybank E	#
1	2	3	4	5	6	7	8	9*	10	11	12														1
1	2	3	4	5	6	7	8		10	11	9														2
1	2	3	4	5	6	7	8		10	11	9														3
	2	3	4	5	6	7	8		10	11	9*		1	12											4
	2	3	4	5	6	7	8	12	9*	11		1	10												5
	2	3	4	5	6		8	9			11	7	1	10											6
	2	3	4		6	7	8				11	9	1	10	5										7
	2	3	4		6	7	8				11	9	1	10	5										8
	2	3	4	5	6		10	8			11	7	1	9											9
	2	3		6	8	4	9	10			11		1		5	7									10
	2	11	4*	5	3	7	8				9		1	10	6	12									11
	2	11	4	6	3	10					7		1	9	5		8								12
	2	11	4	5	3			10			9		1		6		8	7							13
	2		4	5	3	11		8			9		1	10	6			7							14
1	2		4	5	3	11		8		12	9				6		10	7*							15
1	2	10	4	5	3	7					11				8			6	9						16
1	2	10		5	3	7	4				9				8		11	12	6*						17
1	2	10		5	3	7	4				9				8		11	6							18
1	2	12		5	3	8	4				9		11		10		7*	6							19
	2			5	8	4	9				11	7	1	10	6						3				20
	2		4	5	3	7	6	9			11		1	10	8										21
	2		4	5	3	7*	6	9			11		1	10	12		8								22
	2	11	4	5	3		6	9			7		1	10	8										23
	2	12	4	5	3	7	6	9			11		1	10*	8										24
	2	12	4		3	7	6	9			11		1	10	5*		8								25
	2		4		3	7	6	9			11		1	10	8				5						26
	2		4	5		7	6	9			11		1		8						3	10			27
	2*		4	5		7	6				11		1	10	8				12		3	9			28
	2		4	5*	6	7		12			11	10	1		8						3	9			29
	2	12	4*	5	6	10					11		1		8		7				3	9			30
	2		4	5	12	6	10				11		1		8		7				3*	9			31
	2		4	5	6		10				11		1		8		7				3	9			32
	2		4		6		12	10			11		1	5*	8		7				3	9			33
	2		4		6	7	10						1		8		11	5	12		3	9*			34
	2		4	5	10	6					11		1		8		7	9			3				35
	2	10	4	5	3	7	8				11		1					6	9						36
	2		4		3	7	8				11		1	10				6	9			5			37
	2	11	4	5	3	7	8	12					1					6	9			10*			38
	2	11	4	5	3	7	8				9		1	10				6*	12						39
	2			5	6	7					11		1	10	8		4				3	9			40
	2*			5	6	7		12			11		1	10	8		4				3	9			41
			6	7	2						11		1	10	8		4		5		3	9			42
8	41	20	34	26	42	29	34	20	15	10	38	34	21	11	20	4	14	10	5	1	12	9	1	3	
	4				2		2	2	1	1			1	1	1			1		3					
	1	1	5	2		3			4	6		5		7		2		1		1	1	2	1		

23

1975-76

1	Aug	16	(a)	Sunderland	L	1-2	Garner	28,689
2		20	(a)	West Brom A	D	0-0		18,014
3		23	(h)	Carlisle U	W	3-1	Maybank 2, Bason	19,165
4		27	(h)	Oxford U	W	3-1	Wilkins R 2, Swain	22,841
5		30	(a)	Luton T	L	0-3		19,024
6	Sep	6	(h)	Nottingham F	D	0-0		21,023
7		13	(a)	Oldham Ath	L	1-2	Wilkins R	10,406
8		20	(h)	Bristol C	D	1-1	Garner	17,661
9		23	(a)	Portsmouth	D	1-1	Garner	16,144
10		27	(a)	Fulham	L	0-2		22,921
11	Oct	4	(h)	York C	D	0-0		15,323
12		11	(a)	Southampton	L	1-4	Wilkins R	21,227
13		18	(h)	Blackpool	W	2-0	Wilkins R (pen), Langley	16,924
14		25	(a)	Blackburn R	D	1-1	Hutchinson	12,128
15	Nov	1	(h)	Plymouth Argyle	D	2-2	Britton, Wilkins R	20,096
16		8	(a)	Hull C	W	2-1	Britton, Hutchison	9,097
17		15	(h)	Notts Co	W	2-0	Garner, Wilkins R (pen)	18,229
18		22	(a)	Blackpool	W	2-0	Droy, Maybank	8,595
19		29	(a)	Bristol R	W	2-1	Maybank, Hutchinson	16,277
20	Dec	6	(h)	Bolton W	L	0-1		20,896
21		13	(a)	Carlisle U	L	1-2	Wilkins R	8,065
22		22	(h)	Sunderland	W	1-0	Britton	22,802
23		26	(a)	Orient	L	1-3	Maybank	15,509
24		27	(h)	Charlton Ath	L	2-3	Swain, Britton	25,367
25	Jan	10	(h)	Oldham Ath	L	0-3		16,464
26		17	(a)	Nottingham F	W	3-1	Garner, Wilkins R, Hutchinson	14,172
27		31	(h)	West Brom A	L	1-2	Britton	15,896
28	Feb	7	(a)	Oxford U	D	1-1	Garner	11,162
29		18	(h)	Hull C	D	0-0		10,254
30		21	(a)	Notts Co	L	2-3	Stanley, Finnieston	14,528
31		25	(h)	Portsmouth	W	2-0	Cooke, Locke	12,709
32		28	(h)	Blackburn R	W	3-1	Wilkins R 2, Finnieston	14,555
33	Mar	6	(a)	Plymouth Argyle	W	3-0	Stanley, Britton, Swain	20,638
34		13	(h)	Southampton	D	1-1	Finnieston	29,011
35		20	(h)	Bristol R	D	0-0		16,132
36		27	(a)	Bolton W	L	1-2	Britton	20,817
37	Apr	6	(h)	Fulham	D	0-0		23,605
38		10	(a)	Bristol C	D	2-2	Swian, Stanley	24,710
39		16	(h)	Luton T	D	2-2	Finnieston, Hay	19,878
40		17	(h)	Orient	L	0-2		17,679
41		19	(a)	Charlton Ath	D	1-1	Berr (og)	23,263
42		24	(a)	York C	D	2-2	Britton (pen), Finnieston	4,914

FINAL LEAGUE POSITION: 11th in Division Two

Appearances

Sub. Appearances

Goals

24

Sherwood S	Wilkins G	Sparrow J	Stanley G	Droy M	Dempsey J	Britton I	Wilkins R	Maybank E	Garner W	Cooke C	Swain K	Bason B	Harris R	Hay D	Langley T	Hutchinson I	Wicks S	Locke G	Bonnetti P	Finnieston S	Lewington R	Phillips J	
1	2	3	4	5	6	7	8	9	10	11													1
1	2	3	4	5	6	7	8	9	10*	11	12												2
1	2	3		6	5	7*	8	9		11	10	4	12										3
1	2	3		5	6		8	9		11	10	4	7										4
1	2*	3		5	6	7	8	9		11	10	4	12										5
1		3	7	5	4		8	9		11	10		6	2									6
1			4	5	6	7	8		11					2	3	9							7
1			4	6	5	7	8		11		9			2	3		10						8
1			4	5	6	7	8		11		9			2	3		10						9
1			4	5	6	7	8				9*			2	3	11	10	12					10
1		3		6	5	11	8				7			2	4	9	10						11
1			6	5		7	8		11		9*		3	4	12		10	2					12
			6	5		7	8	9*	11				3	4	12		10	2	1				13
			6	5		7	8	9	11				3	4	12		10	2*	1				14
			4	6	5	7	8	9	11				3				10	2	1				15
			4	5	6	7	8	9	11				3				10	2	1				16
			4	5	6	7	8	9	11				3				10	2	1				17
			4	6	5	7	8	9	11*				3			12	10	2	1				18
			4	5	6	7	8	9	11				3				10	2	1				19
			4	6	5	7	8	9		11			3				10	2	1				20
				5	6	7	8	9		11			3	4			10	2	1				21
			4	5	6	7	8	9		11			3			12	10	2	1				22
	12		4	5	6	7	8	9		11			3				10*	2	1				23
			4	5	6*	7	8	9	10	11			3			12		2	1				24
				5		7	8	9	10	11	12		3	4			6*	2	1				25
						7	8	9	10	11		4	3	6			5	2	1				26
						7	8	9	10	11		4	3	6			5	2	1				27
		3				7	8	9	10	11		4	3	6			5	2	1				28
						7	8		10	11		4	3	6			5	2	1	9			29
			4*			7	8		10	11			3	6			5	2	1	9	12		30
			4			7	8		10	11			3	6			5	2	1	9			31
			4			7	8*		10	11			3	6		12	5	2	1	9			32
			4			7	8		10				3	6		12	5	2	1	9	11		33
			4			7	8		10				3	6		12	5	2*	1	9	11		34
	3		4			7	8		10*				2	6		12	5		1	9	11		35
	2		4			7	8		10				3	6			5		1	9	11		36
	3		4			7	8		10				2	6			5		1	9	11		37
	3		4			7	8		10				2	6			5		1	9	11		38
	3		4			7	8		10				2	6		12	5		1*	9	11		39
	3		4			7	8		10				2	6		12	5			9	11*	1	40
	3		4			7	8		10				2	6			5			9	11	1	41
	3*		4			7	8		10				2	6			5			9	11	1	42
12	13	8	29	25	24	40	42	22	21	16	24	8	38	27	4	18	18	23	27	12	8	3	
	1									4	1	1	1	2	1	6	1				1		
			3	1		8	11	5	6		1	4	1	1	1	4	1			5			

25

1976-77

1	Aug	21	(a)	Orient	W	1-0	Finnieston	11,456
2		25	(h)	Notts Co	D	1-1	Britton	17,426
3		28	(h)	Carlisle U	W	2-1	Swain, Finnieston	18,681
4	Sep	4	(a)	Millwall	L	0-3		21,002
5		11	(a)	Plymouth Argyle	W	3-2	Britton (pen), Swain, Finnieston	18,356
6		18	(h)	Bolton W	W	2-1	Hay, Stanley	24,835
7		25	(a)	Blackpool	W	1-0	Finnieston	19,041
8	Oct	2	(h)	Cardiff C	W	2-1	Swain, Lewington	28,409
9		5	(a)	Bristol R	L	1-2	Finnieston	13,199
10		16	(h)	Oldham Ath	W	4-3	Swain, Wilkins R, Wicks, Finnieston	25,825
11		23	(a)	Blackburn R	W	2-0	Finnieston 2 (2 pen)	15,039
12		30	(h)	Southampton	W	3-1	Swian, Finnieston Wilkins R.	42,654
13	Nov	6	(a)	Hereford U	D	2-2	Finnieston 2 (1 pen)	12,858
14		10	(h)	Charlton Ath	W	2-1	Swian, Stanley	38,879
15		20	(a)	Nottingham F	D	1-1	Britton	27,089
16		27	(h)	Burnley	W	2-1	Britton, Finneston (pen)	28,595
17	Dec	3	(a)	Sheffield U	L	0-1		23,393
18		7	(a)	Southampton	D	1-1	Finnieston	19,909
19		11	(h)	Wolverhampton W	D	3-3	Wilkins R, Britton, Finnieston	36,137
20		18	(a)	Hull C	D	1-1	Britton	11,774
21		27	(h)	Fulham	W	2-0	Droy, Swain	55,003
22		29	(a)	Luton T	L	0-4		17,102
23	Jan	1	(h)	Hereford U	W	5-1	Swain, Stanley, Wilkins R 2, Finnieston	27,720
24		22	(h)	Orient	D	1-1	Stanley	25,744
25	Feb	5	(a)	Carlisle U	W	1-0	Swain	11,356
26		12	(h)	Millwall	D	1-1	Stanley	34,857
27		15	(a)	Notts Co	L	1-2	Wilkins R	11,902
28		19	(h)	Plymouth Argyle	D	2-2	Swain, Britton (pen)	22,154
29		26	(a)	Bolton W	D	2-2	Finnieston, Swain	31,600
30	Mar	5	(h)	Blackpool	D	2-2	Swain, Wicks	27,412
31		12	(a)	Cardiff C	W	3-1	Britton, Swain, Stanley	20,194
32		19	(h)	Bristol R	W	2-0	Aitken o.g, Wicks	26,196
33	Apr	2	(h)	Blackburn R	W	3-1	Wicks, Finneston 2	20,769
34		8	(a)	Fulham	L	1-3	Wilkins R	29,690
35		9	(h)	Luton T	W	2-0	Finnieston, Sparrow	31,911
36		11	(a)	Charlton Ath	L	0-4		25,757
37		16	(h)	Nottingham F	W	2-1	Britton, Finnieston	36,499
38		19	(a)	Oldham Ath	D	0-0		10,077
39		23	(a)	Burnley	L	0-0		14,927
40		30	(h)	Sheffield U	W	2-0	Langley, Lewington, Wilkins R, Finnieston	28,158
41	May	7	(a)	Wolverhampton W	D	1-0	Langley	33,465
42		14	(h)	Hull C	W	1-0	Finnieston 3 (1 pen), Britton	43,718

FINAL LEAGUE POSITION: 2nd in Division Two

Appearances

Sub. Appearances

Goals

26

Bonnetti P	Locke G	Wilkins G	Stanley G	Wicks S	Hay D	Britton I	Wilkins R	Finnieston S	Lewington R	Swain K	Bason B	Droy M	Harris R	Cooke C	Phillps J	Sparrow J	Maybank E	Langley T	Walker C	#
1	2	3	4	5	6	7	8	9	10	11										1
1	2	3		5	6	7	8	10	9	11	4									2
1	2	3	4	5	6	7	8	10	9	11										3
1	2	3	4		6	7	8	9*	10	11		5	12							4
1	2	3	4	5	6	7	8	10	9	11										5
1	2	3	4	5	6	7*	8	9	10	11			12							6
1	2	3	4	5	6		8	9	10	11	7									7
1	2	3		5	6		8	9	10	11	7			4						8
1	2	3		5*	6		8	9	10	11	7		12	4						9
1	2	3	4	5	6		8	9	10	11	7									10
1	2	3	4	5			8	9	10	11	7		6							11
	2	3	4	5	6	7	8	9	10	11					1					12
1	2	3	4	5	6	7	8	9	10	11										13
1	2	3	4	5*	6	7	8	9	10	11			12							14
1	2	3	4	5	6	7	8	9	10	11										15
1	2	3	4	5	6	7	8	9	10	11										16
1	2	3	4	5	6	7	8	9	10	11										17
1	2	3	4	5	6	7	8	9	10	11										18
1	2	3	4	5	6	7	8	9	10	11										19
1	2	3	4	5	6	7	8	9	10	11										20
1	2	3	4		6	7	8	9	10	11		5								21
	2	3	4		6	7	8	9	10	11		5			1					22
	2		4*		6	7	8	9	10	11		5	3		1	12				23
	2		4		6	7	8	9	10	11		5	3		1					24
	2		4		6	7	8	9*	10	11		5	3		1	12				25
	2		4		6	7	8		10	11		5	3		1		9			26
	2	3	4		6	7	8		10	11		5			1		9			27
	2	3	4	5	6	7	8		10	11					1		9			28
	2	3	4	5	6	7	8	9	10	11					1					29
	2	3	4	5	6	7	8	9	10	11					1					30
1	2		4	5	6	7	8	9	10	11						3				31
1	2		4	5	6	7	8	9	10	11						3				32
1	2		4	5		7	8	9	10	11			6			3				33
1	2		4	5		7	8	9	10	11			6			3				34
1	2		4	5		7	8	9	10	11			6			3				35
1	2		4	5		7	8	9	10	11			6		1	3				36
1	2			5		7	8	9	10				6	4		3		11		37
1	2			5		7	8	9	10				6	4		3		11		38
1	2			5		7	8	9	10				6	4		3		11*	12	39
1	2			5		7	8	9	10				6	4		3		11		40
1	2			5		7	8	9	10				6	4		3		11		41
1	2			5		7	8	9	10				6	4		3		11		42
31	42	26	33	34	31	37	42	39	42	36	6	8	15	8	11	12	3	6		
													4		2				1	
				4	1	10	8	24	2	13	1				1	2				

1977-78

1	Aug	20	(a)	West Brom A	L 0-3		20,145
2		24	(h)	Birmingham C	W 2-0	Stanley, Lewington	18,008
3		27	(h)	Coventry C	L 1-2	Langley	25,432
4	Sep	3	(a)	Ipswich T	L 0-1		20,835
5		10	(h)	Derby Co	D 1-1	Langley	25,759
6		17	(a)	Manchester U	W 1-0	Garnre	54,764
7		24	(a)	Q.P.R.	D 1-1	Swain	26,267
8	Oct	1	(h)	Leeds U	L 1-2	Wilkins R.	35,427
9		5	(h)	Leicester C	D 0-0		19,575
10		8	(a)	Liverpool	L 0-2		40,499
11		15	(h)	Middlesbrough	D 0-0		21,091
12		22	(a)	Newcastle U	L 0-1		24,000
13		29	(h)	Bristol C	W 1-0	Aylott	22,313
14	Nov	5	(h)	Nottingham F	W 1-0	Aylott	36,116
15		12	(a)	Norwich C	D 0-0		19,566
16		19	(h)	Aston Villa	D 0-0		31,764
17		26	(a)	Manchester C	L 2-6	Wilkins R. Britton (pen)	34,354
18	Dec	3	(h)	Everton	L 0-1		33,899
19		10	(a)	Wolverhampton W	W 3-1	Walker 2, Langley	16,400
20		17	(h)	Norwich C	D 1-1	Wilkins R.	22,751
21		26	(a)	Arsenal	L 0-3		46,074
22		27	(h)	West Ham U	W 2-1	Langley, Garner	44,093
23		31	(a)	Brimingham C	W 5-4	Langley 3, Garner, Walker	19,876
24	Jan	2	(h)	West Brom A	D 2-2	Garner, Walker	29,540
25		14	(a)	Coventry C	L 1-5	Wilkins R.	21,155
26		21	(h)	Ipswich T	W 5-3	Swian 2, Finnieston, Wicks, Langley	26,044
27	Feb	11	(h)	Manchester U	D 2-2	Walker, Wilkins R.	32,238
28		25	(a)	Leeds U	L 0-2		25,263
29	Mar	4	(h)	Liverpool	W 3-1	Langley, Finnieston 2	35,550
30		11	(a)	Derby C	D 1-1	Walker	21,504
31		18	(h)	Newcastle U	D 2-2	Harris, Swain (pen)	22,777
32		21	(a)	Bristol C	L 0-3		19,961
33		25	(a)	West Ham	L 1-3	Garner	24,987
34		27	(h)	Arsenal	D 0-0		40,764
35	Apr	1	(a)	Nottingham F	L 1-3	Langley	31,262
36		4	(a)	Middlesbrough	L 0-2		15,288
37		15	(a)	Aston Villa	L 0-2		27,375
38		22	(h)	Wolverhampton W	D 1-1	Langley	31,637
39		26	(a)	Leicester C	W 2-0	Walker, Wilkins R.	12,170
40		29	(a)	Everton	L 0-6		39,504
41	May	2	(h)	Q.P.R.	W 3-1	Hollins (og), Droy, Lewington	21,201
42		5	(h)	Manchester C	D 0-0		18,782

FINAL LEAGUE POSITION: 16th in Division One

Appearances

Sub. Appearances

Goals

Phillips J	Locke G	Sparrow J	Stanley G	Wicks S	Harris R	Britton	Wilkins R.	Finnieston S	Lewington R	Langley T	Wilkins G.	Droy M	Garner W	Swain K	Bonetti P	Walker C	Aylott T	Cooke C	Hay D	Frost L	No.
1	2	3	4	5	6	7	8	9	10	11											1
1	2	3	4	5	6	7	8	9	10	11											2
1	2	3	4	5	6	7	8	9	10	11											3
1			7	6	2	4	8	9*		11	3	5	12	10							4
1			11	6	2	4	8			9	3	5	12	10							5
1	12		11	6	2	4	8			9	3	5	7*	10							6
1			11	6	2	4	8			9	3	5	7*	10							7
1			11	6	2	4	8			9	3	5	7	10							8
1			11	6	2	4	8		10	9	3	5		7							9
1	12		11*	6	2	4	8			9	3	5	7	10							10
			11*	6	2	4	8			9	3	5	7	10	1	12					11
				6	2	4	8			9*	3	5	7	10	1	11	12				12
				6	2	4	8			9	3	5		10	1	11	7*	11			13
		3		6		4	8			9	2	5		10	1		7	11			14
		3		6		4	8			9	2	5		10	1		7	11			15
		3		6		4	8			9	2	5		10	1		7	11			16
		3		6		4	8		12	9	2	5		10	1		7	11*			17
		3		6	2	4	8		12	9		5		10	1		7	11*			18
		3		6	2	4	8			9		5		10	1		7				19
		3		6	2	4	8			9		5		10	1	11	7				20
		3		6	2	4	8		12	9		5		10	1	11	7				21
				6	2	4		12	8*	9	3	5	7	10	1	11	7*				22
				6	2	4			8	9	3	5	7	10	1	11					23
	12			6	2	4			8	9	3*	5	7	10	1	11					24
		3		6	5	4	8		10	9	2		7		1	11					25
	2			6	3	4	8		12	9		5	7*	10	1	11					26
	2			6	3	4	8		7	9		5		10	1	11					27
	2			6		4	8		7	12	3	5		10	1	11*	9				28
	2			6	3	4	8	10	7	9		5			1	11					29
	2			6	3	4	8	10	7	9		5			1	11					30
	2			6	3	4	8*	10	7	9		5		12	1	11					31
	2			6	3	4		10	7*	9		5	12	8	1				11		32
1	2			6	3	4		10	7	12			9*	8				11	5		33
	2			6	3	4		10	7	9		5		8	1	11					34
	2			6	3	4		10	7	9		5		8	1	11					35
	2			6	3	4		10	7	9		5		8	1	11			5		36
				6	3	4		8	7	9	2		12	10	1				5	11*	37
	2			6		4		10	7	9	3	5	12	8	1						38
	2			6	3			10	8	9		5	7		1	11			4		39
	2			6	3		8	10	7	9		5		4	1	11					40
	2			6	3	4		10	7	12		5	9*	8	1	11					41
				6	3	4		10	7	9		5		8	1	11			2		42
11	18	12	11	41	37	40	33	18	20	39	21	35	15	35	31	21	10	6	7	1	
	3							2	4	2		3	1			2	1				
		1	1	1	1	6	3	2		11	1	5	4				7	2			

1978-79

1	Aug	19	(h)	Everton	L	0-1		31,755
2		22	(a)	Wolverhampton W	W	1-0	Langley	22,041
3		26	(a)	Tottenham H	D	2-2	Swain 2	40,643
4	Sep	2	(h)	Leeds U	L	0-3		30,099
5		9	(a)	Coventry C	L	2-3	Langley, McKenzie	24,920
6		16	(h)	Manchester C	L	1-4	Stanley	28,980
7		23	(a)	Birmingham C	D	1-1	McKenzie	18,458
8		30	(h)	West Brom A	L	1-3	Wicks	20,186
9	Oct	7	(a)	Derby Co	L	0-1		20,251
10		14	(h)	Bolton W	W	4-3	Langley, Swain, Walker, Allardyce (og)	19,879
11		21	(a)	Liverpool	L	0-2		45,775
12		28	(h)	Norwich C	W	3-2	Swain, Walker, Stanley (pen)	23,941
13	Nov	4	(a)	Q.P.R.	D	0-0		22,878
14		11	(a)	Everton	L	2-3	McKenzie, Langley	38,694
15		18	(h)	Tottenham H	L	1-3	Langley	41,594
16		22	(a)	Leeds U	L	1-2	Langley	24,088
17		25	(h)	Manchester U	L	0-1		27,156
18	Dec	9	(h)	Aston Villa	L	0-1		19,080
19		16	(a)	Middlesbrough	L	2-7	Osgood, Bumstead	15,107
20		23	(h)	Bristol C	D	0-0		19,093
21		26	(a)	Southampton	D	0-0		20,770
22		30	(a)	Ipswich T	L	1-5	Langley	21,439
23	Jan	20	(a)	Manchester C	W	3-2	McKenzie, Osgood, Walker	31,876
24	Feb	3	(h)	Birmingham C	W	2-1	Wilkins (R) 2	22,129
25		21	(h)	Coventry C	L	1-3	Langley	15,282
26		24	(a)	Bolton W	L	1-2	Bannon	19,457
27	Mar	3	(h)	Liverpool	D	0-0		40,594
28		10	(a)	Norwich C	L	0-2		19,071
29		14	(a)	West Brom A	L	0-1		20,425
30		17	(h)	Q.P.R.	L	1-3	Shanks (og)	25,871
31		24	(h)	Wolverhampton	L	1-2	Langley	20,502
32		28	(a)	Nottingham F	L	0-6		24,514
33	Apr	4	(h)	Derby Co	D	1-1	Langley	10,682
34		7	(h)	Nottingham F	L	1-3	Wilkins (R)	29,213
35		10	(a)	Bristol C	L	1-3	Langley (pen)	18,645
36		14	(h)	Southampton	L	1-2	Stanley	18,243
37		16	(a)	Arsenal	L	2-5	Walker, Langley	37,232
38		21	(h)	Middlesbrough	W	2-1	Stanley, Wilkins (G)	12,007
39		28	(a)	Aston Villa	L	1-2	Langley	29,219
40	May	5	(h)	Ipswich T	L	2-3	Langley 2	15,462
41		14	(h)	Arsenal	D	1-1	Stanley	28,386
42		16	(a)	Manchester U	D	1-1	Johnson	38,119

FINAL LEAGUE POSITION: 22nd in Division One

Appearances

Sub. Appearances

Goals

Bonetti P	Locke G	Harris R	Hay D	Droy M	Wicks S	Swain K	Wilkins R	Langley T	Stanley G	Walker C	Britton I	Lewington R	McKenzie D	Stride D	Iles R	Garner W	Phillips J	Wilkins G	Bumstead J	Aylott T	Osgood P	Nutton M	Bannon E	Sitton J	Borota P	Doherty J	Frost L	Fillery M	Chivers G	Johnson G	
1	2	3	4	5	6	7	8	9*	10	11	12																				1
1	2	3	4	5	6	7	8	9	10	11																					2
1	2	3	4	5	6	7	8	9	10	11																					3
1	2	3	4	5	6	7	8	9	10	11																					4
1	2	3		5	6	7	8	9	10*		12	4	11																		5
1	2	3		5	6	7	8*	9	10		12	4	11																		6
1	2	6			5	7	8	9	4			10	11	3																	7
1	2	6			5	7	8	9	4	12		10	11*	3																	8
		6	2		5	7	8	9			4		10	3	1	11															9
		4	2		5	11	10	9	8*		12		7	6	3	1															10
		6			5	10	8*	9	4	11	12		7	3	1			2													11
		6			5	10	8	9	4	11			7	3	1			2													12
		6			5	10	8	9	4	11			7	3	1			2													13
		6			5	10	8	9	4	11			7	3	1			2													14
		6			5	10	8	9	4	11			7	3	1			2													15
		6			5		8	9	4	12		11	7*	3			1	2		10											16
		6			5		8	9	4	11		10	7	3			1	2													17
		6			5		8		4	12		11	7*	3			1	2		10	9										18
		6			5		8			11	12		7	3			1	2	4	10	9*										19
		2			5			10	7	11			8	3			1					6	9	4							20
		2			5			10	7*	11			8	3			1				12	6	9	4							21
		2			5			9	7*	12		10	8	3			1					6	11	4							22
1		4		5	6			10	7	11			8	3				2			9										23
1		12		5*				8	10	7	11			3				2			9	6	4								24
1		5*						8	10	7	11			3				2			9	6	4	12							25
1								8	10	7	11			3				2			9	6	4	5							26
				9				8	10	7*	11			3				2				6	4	5	1			12			27
				9				8	10*		11			3				2	12	7		6	4	5	1						28
				9				8	10		11			3*				2	12			6	4	5	1	7					29
				9				8	12	10	11			3				2				6	4	5	1	7*					30
				7				8	10	12	11			3*				2			9	6	4	5	1						31
				7				8	10	12	11			3				2*			9	6	4	5	1						32
				7	5			8	10		11*			3				2				6	4		1		9	12			33
				7	5			8	10	12				3				2			9	6	4		1			11*			34
				7	5			8	10					3				2			9	6	4		1			11			35
					6			8	7	12				3				2		10	9*		4	5	1			11			36
					5			8	10	11	12			3				2			9*		4	6	1			7			37
1		12			5			8	10	7	11			3*				2					4				9		6		38
1		3			5			8	10	7	11							2	12				4					9*	6		39
1		3			5			8	10	7											9		4				12	11*	6		40
1		3			5				10	7	11									8	9		4	6					2		41
		3							10		11							2		7	8		4	5	1				6	9	42
16	8	38	8	14	23	15	35	40	32	23	9	10	15	32	7	1	7	28	6	13	9	15	19	11	12	2	2	6	5	1	
	2						1	4	7	4				4				2	2					1		1	1	1			
		1		4	3	15	5	4			4					1	1		2		1									1	

1979-80

#	Month	Date		Opponent	Result	Score	Scorers	Attendance
1	Aug	18	(h)	Sunderland	D	0-0		23,500
2		20	(a)	West Ham U	W	1-0	Johnson	31,627
3		25	(h)	Wrexham	W	3-1	Harris, Britton, Bumstead	18,732
4	Sep	1	(a)	Newcastle U	L	1-2	Fillery	25,230
5		8	(h)	Birmingham C	L	1-2	Walker	17,182
6		15	(a)	Shrewsbury T	L	0-3		9,271
7		22	(h)	Watford	W	2-0	Johnson 2	21,480
8		29	(a)	Cambridge U	W	1-0	Johnson	8,792
9	Oct	6	(a)	Burnley	W	1-0	Langley	8,341
10		13	(h)	Bristol R	W	1-0	Chivers	18,236
11		20	(a)	Cardiff C	W	2-1	Frost, Fillery	16,328
12		27	(h)	Fulham	L	0-2		30,567
13	Nov	3	(a)	Sunderland	L	1-2	Johnson	24,988
14		10	(a)	Orient	W	7-3	Britton, Frost 3, Fillery, Walker 2	13,005
15		14	(h)	West Ham U	W	2-1	Frost, Fillery	30,859
16		17	(h)	Charlton Ath	W	3-1	Fillery, Britton 2(2 pens)	23,035
17		24	(a)	Notts Co	W	3-2	Britton, Walker 2	12,646
18	Dec	1	(h)	Preston NE	W	2-0	Droy, Britton	21,192
19		8	(a)	Oldham Ath	L	0-1		10,201
20		15	(h)	Swansea C	W	3-0	Bumstead, Langley, Johnson	18,065
21		18	(a)	Q.P.R.	D	2-2	Langley, Bumstead	26,598
22		26	(h)	Leicester C	W	1-0	Fillery	25,320
23		29	(a)	Wrexham	L	0-2		15,641
24	Jan	1	(a)	Luton T	D	3-3	Fillery, Britton, Walker	19,717
25		12	(h)	Newcastle U	W	4-0	Fillery, Barton (og), Langley, Walker	32,281
26	Feb	2	(h)	Shrewsbury T	L	2-4	Langley 2	18,120
27		9	(a)	Watford	W	3-2	Britton, Johnson, Walker	24,716
28		16	(h)	Cambridge U	D	1-1	Fillery	17,112
29		23	(a)	Bristol R	L	0-3		14,176
30	Mar	1	(h)	Cardiff C	W	1-0	Walker	18,449
31		8	(a)	Fulham	W	2-1	Walker 2	22,348
32		11	(a)	Birmingham C	L	1-5	Langley	27,297
33		15	(h)	Burnley	W	2-1	Harris, Langley	16,189
34		22	(h)	Orient	W	1-0	Britton	19,706
35		29	(a)	Charlton Ath	W	2-1	Britton, Langley	16,425
36	Apr	2	(h)	Q.P.R.	L	0-2		31,035
37		5	(a)	Leicester C	L	0-1		25,826
38		7	(h)	Luton T	D	1-1	Lee	28,078
39		12	(a)	Preston NE	D	1-1	Fillery	13,069
40		19	(h)	Notts Co	W	1-0	Chivers	24,002
41		26	(a)	Swansea C	D	1-1	Langley	16,000
42	May	3	(h)	Oldham Ath	W	3-0	Fillery, Walker 2	28,253

FINAL LEAGUE POSITION: 4th in Division Two

Appearances

Sub. Appearances

Goals

32

Borota P	Locke G	Wilkins G	Nutton M	Droy M	Harris R	Britton I	Bannon E	Langley T	Johnson G	Fillery M	Stride D	Aylott T	Bumstead J	Chivers G	Sitton J	Walker C	Osgood P	Frost L	Hales K	Pates C	Sparrow J	Rhoades-Brown P	Iles R	Rofe D	Lee C	Viljoen C	
1	2	3	4	5	6	7	8	9	10	11																	1
1	2		4	5	6	7	8	9	10	11	3																2
1	2	4		5	6	7	8	9		11	3	10*	12														3
1		3		5	6	7	4	9		10		11*	8	2	12												4
1	2	3	6	5				9		11		10	4	12		7	8*										5
1	2	3	6	5		7	8*	9	10	11			4	12													6
1	2	3*	6	5	12	7		9	10	8			4	11													7
1	2	3	6*	5	11	7		9	8	10			4	12													8
1	2	3		5	11	7		9	10	8			4*	6	12												9
1	2			5	11	7		9	10	8	3		4	6													10
1	2	3		5	11	7			10	8			4	6			9										11
1	2	3		5	11	7	6*	9	10	8			4	12													12
1	2	3		5*	11	7		9	10	8			4	6	12												13
1	2	3			9	7			10				4*	5	11		8	12	6								14
1	2			5	11	7				8			4	6		10	9			3							15
1	2			5	11	7		12		8			4	6		10	9				3*						16
1	2	3		5	11	7				8			4	6		10	9										17
1	2	3		5	11	7				8			4	6		10	9										18
1	2	3		5	11	7				8			4	6		10	9										19
1	2				11	7		9	12	8			4	6		10*			5	3							20
1	2				11	7		9		8			4	6		10			5	3							21
1	2			5	11	7		9		8			4	6		10				3							22
1	2			5	11*	7		9		8			4	6		10				3		12					23
1	2				9	7			10	8			6	4		11			5	3							24
1	2			5	11	7		9		8			4	6		10				3							25
1	2			5	11	7		9	12	8			4*	6		10				3							26
1	2			5	6	7		9	10	8			4			11				3							27
1	2				6	7		9	11	8			4			10			12	5	3*						28
	2				11	7		4		8			6			10	9		5			1	3				29
1	2		6		11	7		9		8					12		4*		5				3	10			30
1		2	6	5	11	7		9		8					4			12					3	10*			31
1		2	6	5	11	7		9	12	8					10		4*						3				32
1		2	4		11	7		9		8					10				5				3		6		33
1	2		6	5	11	7		9*		8					10			12					3		4		34
1	2		6		11	7		9		8				12	10		4		5	8*			3				35
1	2		6		11	7		9		8					10		4*		5	12			3				36
1			6			7		9		8				2	10		4*		5	12			3		11		37
1			6		11	7		9	12					2	10				5				3*	8	4		38
1			6		11	7		9		8				4	2			12	5				3	10*			39
1			6		11	7		9		8				4	2		10*		5				3		12		40
1			6	12	11*	7		9		8				4	2		10		5				3				41
1			6	12	11	7		9		8				4*	2		10		5				3				42
41	32	18	19	26	38	41	6	35	12	40	3	3	27	27	29	1	8	5	16	11	1	1	14	4	4		
			2	1			1	3	1			1	2	1	7		2	2			3			1			
			1	2	11		10	7	11			3	2		15		5								1		

1980-81

1	Aug	16	(h)	Wrexham	D	2-2	Rhoades-Brown, Fillery	20,001
2		20	(a)	Derby Co	L	2-3	Walker, Johnson	20,353
3		23	(a)	Shrewsbury T	D	2-2	Walker, Fillery	6,672
4		30	(h)	Q.P.R.	D	1-1	Chivers	23,381
5	Sept	6	(h)	West Ham U	L	0-1		32,669
6		13	(a)	Cambridge U	W	1-0	Lee	9,474
7		20	(h)	Preston NE	D	1-1	Lee	13,755
8		27	(a)	Watford	W	3-2	Walker 2, Lee	19,802
9	Oct	4	(a)	Bolton W	W	3-2	Lee 2, Fillery	11,888
10		8	(h)	Bristol R	W	2-0	Lee (og), Walker	13,108
11		11	(h)	Grimsby T	W	3-0	Lee 2, Walker	16,206
12		18	(a)	Blackburn R	D	1-1	Walker	15,503
13		21	(a)	Orient	W	1-0	Fillery	11,950
14		25	(h)	Newcastle U	W	6-0	Lee 3, Fillery, Walker, Chivers	22,912
15		31	(a)	Cardiff C	W	1-0	Hutchings	8,489
16	Nov	8	(h)	Oldham Ath	W	1-0	Lee	19,327
17		12	(h)	Derby Co	L	1-3	Lee	19,449
18		15	(a)	Wrexham	W	4-0	Britton, Driver, Walker, Lee	7,953
19		22	(h)	Sheffield Wednesday	W	2-0	Lee, Walker	24,947
20		29	(a)	Notts Co	D	1-1	Bumstead	14,419
21	Dec	6	(h)	Swansea C	D	0-0		20,067
22		13	(a)	Grimsby T	L	0-2		14,708
23		20	(h)	Orient	L	0-1		15,943
24		26	(a)	Luton T	L	0-2		16,006
25		27	(h)	Bristol C	D	0-0		18,514
26	Jan	10	(a)	Sheffield Wednesday	D	0-0		25,113
27		17	(a)	QPR	L	0-1		22,873
28		31	(h)	Shrewsbury T	W	3-0	Mayes, Lee (pen), Fillery	14,673
29	Feb	7	(h)	Cambridge U	W	3-0	Droy, Mayes 2	16,704
30		14	(a)	West Ham U	L	0-4		35,164
31		21	(h)	Watford	L	0-1		19,153
32		28	(a)	Preston NE	L	0-1		8,129
33	Mar	7	(h)	Bolton W	W	2-0	Walker, Mayes	12,948
34		14	(a)	Bristol R	L	0-1		7,565
35		21	(h)	Blackburn R	D	0-0		14,314
36		28	(a)	Newcastle U	L	0-1		17,392
37	Apr	4	(h)	Cardiff C	L	0-1		11,569
38		11	(a)	Oldham Ath	D	0-0		6,740
39		18	(a)	Bristol C	D	0-0		9,764
40		20	(h)	Luton T	L	0-2		12,868
41		25	(a)	Swansea C	L	0-3		16,063
42	May	2	(h)	Notts Co	L	0-2		13,324

FINAL LEAGUE POSITION: 12th in Division Two

Appearances

Sub. Appearances

Goals

Borota	Wilkins	Rofe	Bumstead	Droy	Chivers	Briton	Fillery	Johnson	Walker	Rhoades-Brown	Viljoen	Nutton	Pates	Lee	Driver	Hutchings	Locke	Elmes	Mayes	Clare	
1	2	3	4	5	6	7	8	9*	10	11	12										1
1	2	3	4	5	6	7	8	9	10	11											2
1	2	3	4	5	6	7	8	9*	10	12		11									3
1	2	3	12		6	7	8		10*		4	11	5	9							4
1	2	3	4*	12		7	8		10			11	5	6	9						5
1	2	3	4	5	11	7	8		10					6	9						6
1	2	3	4	5	11	7	8*		10	12				6	9						7
1	2	3	4	5	6	7	8		10	11					9						8
1	2	3	4		6	7	8		10*	11			5	9					12		9
1	2	3	4		6	7*	8		10	11			5	9	12						10
1	2	3	4		6	7	8		10	11			5*	9	12						11
1		3	4		6	7*	8		10	11		2	5	9	12						12
1		3	4		6		8		10	11		2	5	9	7						13
1		3	4	5	6	12	8		10*	11		2		9	7						14
1		3	4	5	6		8*		10	11		2		9	7	12					15
1		3	4	5	6				10	11		2		9	7	8					16
1		3	4	5	6*		8		10	11		2		9	7	12					17
1	2	3	4	5		7			10	11		6*		9	12	8					18
1		3	4	5	6	7			10	11		2*		9	12	8					19
1		3	4	5	6		8		10	11				9	7		2				20
1		3	4	5	6		8		10	11				9	7		2				21
1		3	4	5	6	7	8		10	11*				9	12		2				22
1		3*	4	5	6	7	8		10	11				9	12		2				23
1		3	6			7						5*	4	10	9	8	2	12	11		24
1		3	4		6		8	12	11			5		9		7*	2		10		25
1		3		5	6	7	8		10	11*				9	12		2	4			26
1		3	4	5	6	7	8		10	11*							2	12	9		27
1		3	4	5	6		8		10		7			9			2		11		28
1		3	4	5	6		8		10		7			9			2		11		29
1		3	4	5	6		8			11				9	12		2	7*	10		30
1		3	4*	5	6		8	12	11	7				9			2		10		31
1		3	4	5	6	7	8	10	9		11*				12		2				32
1		3	4	5	6	7*	8		10	11					12		2		9		33
1		3	4	5	6	7	8		10	11*					12		2		9		34
1		3	4	5	6	7	8		10	11*		12					2		9		35
1		3	4	5	6		8*		10	11				9	7	12	2				36
1		3	4	5	6		8		10	11				9	7		2				37
1			4	5	6		8					2	3	9	7	11			10		38
1			4	5*	2		8					6	3	9	7	11	12		10		39
1		3	4		6		8			12		5	2	9		11	7		10*		40
1	3		4		6		8	12	10	11		5*	2	9		7					41
1	3		4		6	7	8		10	12	11	5		9		2*					42
42	14	38	40	30	39	27	35	3	35	30	6	18	15	34	12	8	21	2	13		
			1		1	1	1		2	4	1			11	1	4	1	2		1	
			1	1	2	1	6	1	11	1		15	1	1				4			

35

1981-82

1	Aug	29	(h)	Bolton W	W	2-0	Lee, Droy	16,606
2	Sept	5	(a)	Cardiff C	W	2-1	Mayes 2	8,898
3		12	(h)	Watford	L	1-3	Walker	20,036
4		19	(a)	Shrewsbury T	L	0-1		5,616
5		23	(h)	Charlton Ath	D	2-2	Driver 2	15,329
6		26	(h)	Norwich C	W	2-1	Bumstead (pen), Driver	14,509
7		28	(a)	Orient	W	2-0	Fillery, Mayes	9,698
8	Oct	3	(a)	Cambridge U	L	0-1		8,806
9		10	(h)	Wrexham	W	2-0	Fillery, Lee	14,170
10		16	(a)	Leicester C	D	1-1	Fillery	18,385
11		24	(h)	Barnsley	L	1-2	Mayes	15,268
12		31	(a)	Rotherham U	L	0-6		10,145
13	Nov	7	(h)	Newcastle U	W	2-1	Lee, Fillery	16,059
14		14	(a)	Oldham Ath	L	0-1		9,773
15		21	(h)	Grimsby T	D	1-1	Lee	11,931
16		24	(a)	Charlton Ath	W	4-3	Walker 2, Bumstead 2	11,082
17		28	(a)	Derby Co	D	1-1	Walker	13,963
18	Dec	5	(h)	Sheffield Wednesday	W	2-1	Hales, Lee	17,033
19		19	(h)	Blackburn R	D	1-1	Lee	11,768
20		26	(a)	QPR	W	2-0	Walker, Mayes	22,022
21	Jan	16	(a)	Bolton W	D	2-2	Mayes, Bumstead	7,278
22		30	(h)	Shrewsbury T	W	3-1	Walker 3	11,446
23	Feb	6	(a)	Watford	L	0-1		17,101
24		17	(h)	Cardiff C	W	1-0	Walker	9,710
25		20	(a)	Norwich C	L	1-2	Walker	16,018
26		27	(a)	Wrexham	L	0-1		3,935
27	Mar	9	(h)	Leicester C	W	4-1	Hales, Locke, Mayes 2	10,586
28		12	(a)	Barnsley	L	1-2	Lee	12,706
29		17	(h)	Crystal Palace	L	1-2	Mayes	13,894
30		20	(h)	Rotherham U	L	1-4	Rhoades-Brown	11,900
31		27	(a)	Newcastle U	L	0-1		26,887
32	Apr	3	(h)	Oldham Ath	D	2-2	Mayes 2	8,938
33		7	(h)	Cambridge U	W	4-1	Hutchings, Lee 2, Fillery	6,196
34		10	(h)	QPR	W	2-1	Droy, Lee	18,365
35		12	(a)	Crystal Palace	W	1-0	Walker	17,189
36		17	(a)	Grimsby T	D	3-3	Walker 3	9,164
37		20	(a)	Luton T	D	2-2	Walker, Fillery	16,185
38		24	(h)	Derby Co	L	0-2		11,005
39	May	1	(a)	Sheffield Wednesday	D	0-0		19,259
40		5	(h)	Orient	D	2-2	Lee, Mayes	6,009
41		8	(h)	Luton T	L	1-2	Walker	15,044
42		15	(a)	Blackburn R	D	1-1	Pates	6,133

FINAL LEAGUE POSITION: 12th in Division Two

Appearances

Sub. Appearances

Goals

Borota P	Locke G	Rofe D	Vijoen C	Droy M	Pates C	Walker C	Bumstead J	Lee C	Mayes A	Fillery M	Driver P	Chivers G	Iles R	Rhoades-Brown P	Hutchings C	Britton I	Wilkins G	Francis S	Hales K	Nutton M	Canoville P	No.
1	2	3	4	5	6	7	8*	9	10	11	12											1
1	2	3	4	5*	6	7	8	9	10	11	12											2
1	2	3	4		5*	7	8	9	10	11	12	6										3
1	2	3	4		5	7	8	9	10*	11	12	6										4
	2	3*	4	5		8	9	10	11	7		6	1	12								5
1	2			5		8	9	10	11	7		6		4	3							6
1	2			5		8	9	10	11	7		6		4	3							7
1	2			5	12	8	9	10	11	7*		6		4	3							8
1	2		4	5			9	10	11			6		7	3	8						9
1	2		4	5	12		9	10*	11			6		7	3	8						10
1	2		4	5	12		9	10	11			6		7	·3	8*						11
1			4	5	6	10	8	9	12	11		2		7*	3							12
1			4			11	7	10	9	3		6		5	8	2						13
				12	5	10	8	9	11			6		7	3	4*	2	1				14
				5	6	10	8	9	12	11				7	3	4*	2	1				15
				5	6	10	8	9	7	11					3		2	1	4			16
				5	6	10	8	9	7	11					3		2	1	4			17
				5	6	10	8	9	7	11				12	3		2*	1	4			18
				5	6	10	8	9	7	11					3		2	1	4			19
				5	6	10	8	9	7	11					3		2	1	4			20
				5	6	10	8	9	7	11					3		2	1	4			21
	2			5	6	8		10	7	11*		9		4	3			1		12		22
	2			5	6	8*	9	10	7	11		12			3			1	4			23
	2			5	6		9	10	7	11					3		8	1	4			24
	2			5*	6		9	10	12	11				7	3		8	1	4			25
	2			5	6		9	10	12	11				7	3	8*		1	4			26
	2			5	6		9	10		11				7	3		8	1	4			27
	2			5	6		9	10		11		12		7	3		8*	1	4			28
	2			5	6*		9	10		11		12		7	3	8		1	4			29
	2			5	6		9	10		11		12		7	3	8*		1	4			30
	2		8	5	6		9	10		11		12		7*	3			1	4			31
	2			5	6	8	9	10		11				7	3			1	4			32
				5	6	8	9*	10		11		12		7	3		2	1	4			33
	3			5	6	8	9	10		11		12		7*			2	1	4			34
	2			5	6	8*	9	10		11				7	3			1	4	12		35
	2			5	6	8	9	10		11				7	3			1	4			36
	2			5	6	8	9	10		11				7	3			1	4			37
	2			5	6	8*	9	10		11				12	3	7		1	4			38
	2	12		5	6	8	9	10		11				7	3			1	4*			39
	2	3*		5	6	7	9	10		11		12			4	8		1				40
	2		4	5	6	8	9	10		11				7*	3			1		12		41
	2		4	5	6	8*	9	10		11					3			1		12	7	42
12	31	6	9	20	42	31	21	40	35	39	4	28	1	24	35	17	10	29	10	17	1	
	1		3	5					4	1		4	1		3	1	1			2	2	
1			2	1	16	4	11	12	6	3					1	1		2				

1982-83

1	Aug	28	(a)	Cambridge U	W	1-0	Robson	8,124
2		31	(h)	Wolverhampton W	D	0-0		14,192
3	Sep	4	(h)	Leicester C	D	1-1	Droy	8,075
4		8	(a)	Derby Co	L	0-1		8,075
5		11	(a)	Newcastle U	D	1-1	Lee	29,084
6		18	(h)	Oldham Ath	W	2-0	Speedie 2	10,263
7		25	(a)	Sheffield W	L	2-3	Fillery (pen), Lee	18,833
8	Oct	2	(h)	Grimsby T	W	5-2	Fillery, Speedie 2, Droy, Bumstead	10,019
9		9	(h)	Leeds U	D	0-0		25,358
10		16	(a)	Blackburn R	L	0-3		6,062
11		23	(h)	Charlton Ath	W	3-1	Bumstead, Pates, Robson	14,492
12		30	(a)	Carlisle U	L	1-2	Lee	7,141
13	Nov	6	(h)	Crystal Palace	D	0-0		15,169
14		13	(a)	Barnsley	D	1-1	Fillery	13,286
15		20	(h)	Shrewsbury T	L	1-2	Lee	8,690
16		27	(a)	Rotherham U	L	0-1		8,793
17	Dec	4	(h)	Burnley	W	2-1	Speedie, Droy	8,184
18		11	(a)	Middlesbrough	L	1-3	Fillery (pen)	8,836
19		18	(h)	Bolton W	W	2-1	Deakin (og), Pates	6,903
20		27	(a)	Q.P.R.	W	2-1	Walker, Speedie	23,744
21		28	(h)	Fulham	D	0-0		29,797
22	Jan	1	(a)	Shrewsbury T	L	0-2		7,545
23		3	(a)	Leicester C	L	0-3		13,745
24		15	(h)	Cambridge U	W	6-0	Jones, Fillery 2, Bumstead, Murray (og), Mayes	7,808
25		22	(h)	Wolverhampton W	L	1-2	Pates	19,533
26	Feb	5	(h)	Derby Co	L	1-3	Pates	8,661
27		12	(a)	Grimsby T	L	1-2	Mayes	6,711
28		19	(a)	Leeds U	D	3-3	Walker, Fillery (pen), Gray E. (og)	19,365
29		26	(h)	Blackburn R	W	2-0	Walker, Rhoades-Brown	6,982
30	Mar	5	(a)	Charlton Ath	L	2-5	Robson, Lee	11,211
31		12	(h)	Carlisle U	W	4-2	Walker, Bumstead, Canoville 2	6,677
32		19	(a)	Crystal Palace	D	0-0		13,437
33		26	(h)	Barnsley	L	0-3		7,223
34	Apr	2	(a)	Fulham	D	1-1	Canoville	15,249
35		4	(h)	Q.P.R.	L	0-2		20,821
36		9	(a)	Oldham Ath	D	2-2	Fillery 2 (1 pen)	4,973
37		16	(h)	Newcastle U	L	0-2		13,446
38		23	(a)	Burnley	L	0-3		7,393
39		30	(h)	Rotherham U	D	1-1	Walker	8,674
40	May	2	(h)	Sheffield W	D	1-1	Speedie	10,462
41		7	(a)	Bolton W	W	1-0	Walker	8,687
42		14	(h)	Middlesbrough	D	0-0		19,340

FINAL LEAGUE POSITION: 18th in Division Two

Appearances

Sub. Appearances

Goals

Francis S	Nutton M	Huchings C	Chivers G	Droy M	Pates C	Walker C	Bumstead J	Lee C	Robson B	Fillery M	Canoville P	McAndrew A	Driver P	Speedie D	Locke G	Rhoades-Brown R	Mayes A	Jones J	Falco M	Hales K	Iles R	Williams P	Jones K	No.
1	2	3	4	5	6	7*	8	9	10	11	12													1
1	2	3	4	5	6	7	8	9	10	11														2
1	2	3	4	5	6		8	9	10	11		7												3
1	2	3	4	5	6*		8	9	10	11	12	7												4
1	2	3	4	5			8	9	10*	11	7	6	12											5
1	2	3	4	5			8	9	12	11	7*	6		10										6
1	2	3	4	5			8	9	12	11	7*	6		10										7
1		3	4	5		9	8	2		11	7	6		10										8
1		3	5	4		9	8*	12		11	7	6		10	2									9
1		3	5	4			8	12		11	7			10	2	6*	9							10
1		3	6	5	4	7	8	9		11				10	2									11
1		3	5	4		7	8	12	9*					10	2	11	6							12
1		3	6	5	4	7	8	12	9*	11				10	2									13
1		3	6	5	4	9	8			11				10	2	7								14
1		6	5	4			8	9		11			12	10		7	3	2*						15
1		3	5	4	6			12		11	7			9*		8	2	10						16
1		3	5	4	6			12		11	7			9		8*	2	10						17
1		3	5	4	6			12		11	7			9		8*	2	10						18
1		3	4	5	6	12	8	7*	9	11				10				2						19
1		3	4	5	6	7	8	9		11				10				2						20
1		3	4	5	6	7	8	12	9	11				10*				2						21
1		3	4	5	6	7*	8	12	10	11				9				2						22
1		3	4	5	6	7	8	12	10	11*				9				2						23
1			4	5		12	8*	2		11	7			10		9	3	6						24
1		6	5	4		12		2		11	7			10		9*	3			8				25
1		6	5		4		8	2	10		7		12	9		11*	3							26
1			5	4	6		8*	2		11	7			10		9	3							27
1*			5	12	6		8	2		11	7	4		10		9	3							28
1		3	5	4	6		8	2		11	7*			10		9								29
1		3	5	4	6		8	12	10	11	7*					9		2						30
		3	5	4	6	7	8	9		11				10				2			1			31
1		3	5	4	6	7	8	9		11				10				2						32
1		3	5	4	6		8*	2		11				10		9		12	7					33
		3	5	4	6	7	8	9		11				10				2			1			34
		3	5	4	6	7	8	9		11				10*			12	2			1			35
		3		4	6	7	8			11				10		9		2			1	5		36
		3	5	4	6	7	8			11*				10		9		2	12		1			37
1		3	5	4	6		8			11	7			10		9*	12	2						38
1		3	4	5	6		8			11	7			10		9	12	2*						39
1		3	4	5	6		8			11	7			10		9		2						40
1		3	4	5	6		8			11	7			10		9		2						41
1		3	4	5	6		8			11	7			10		9		2						42
37	8	36	29	31	35	23	35	31	11	36	16	7	9	34	6	25	13	28	3	3	5	1	0	
		1			6	1	4	4	1	3			4		1			2						
			3	4	6	4	5	3	9	3			7		1	2	1							

1983-84

1	Aug	27	(h)	Derby Co	W	5-0	Spackman, Hutchings, Walker, Dixon 2	17,338
2	Sep	3	(a)	Brighton & HA	W	2-1	Dixon 2	20,874
3		7	(a)	Blackburn R	D	0-0		5,873
4		10	(h)	Cambridge U	W	2-1	Bumstead, Walker	14,425
5		17	(a)	Sheffield W	L	1-2	Walker	20,596
6		24	(h)	Middlesbrough	D	0-0		15,822
7	Oct	1	(a)	Huddersfield T	W	3-2	Dixon 2, Canoville	13,280
8		8	(a)	Fulham	W	5-3	Nevin, Lee, Dixon 2, Jones	24,787
9		15	(h)	Cardiff C	W	2-0	Nevin, Lee	15,459
10		22	(a)	Carlisle U	D	0-0		6,774
11		29	(h)	Charlton Ath	W	3-2	Speedie 2, Dixon	17,789
12	Nov	5	(a)	Oldham Ath	D	1-1	Bumstead	5,807
13		12	(h)	Newcastle U	W	4-0	Spackman, Rhoades-Brown, Speedie 2	30,628
14		15	(a)	Charlton Ath	D	1-1	Nevin	14,393
15		19	(h)	Crystal Palace	D	2-2	Hollins, Speedie	19,060
16		22	(a)	Swansea C	W	3-1	Bumstead, Nevin, Dixon	7,848
17		26	(a)	Leeds U	D	1-1	Dixon	20,680
18	Dec	3	(h)	Manchester C	L	0-1		29,142
19		6	(h)	Swansea C	W	6-1	Canoville 3, Nevin, Dixon, Bumstead	12,389
20		10	(a)	Barnsley	D	0-0		10,300
21		17	(h)	Grimsby T	L	2-3	Dixon (pen), Bumstead	13,151
22		26	(a)	Shrewsbury T	W	4-2	Dixon (pen), Speedie, Bumstead 2	7,582
23		27	(h)	Portsmouth	D	2-2	Dixon, Canoville	25,440
24		31	(h)	Brighton & HA	W	1-0	Speedie	18,542
25	Jan	2	(a)	Middlesbrough	L	1-2	McAndrew	11,579
26		14	(a)	Derby Co	W	2-1	Cherry (og), McAndrew (pen)	16,727
27		21	(h)	Sheffield W	W	3-2	Thomas 2, Nevin	35,147
28	Feb	4	(h)	Huddersfield T	W	3-1	Dixon 2, Speedie	17,922
29		11	(a)	Cambridge U	W	1-0	McAndrew	10,602
30		25	(h)	Carlisle U	D	0-0		16,543
31	Mar	3	(h)	Oldham Ath	W	3-0	Speedie, Dixon, McAndrew (pen)	12,736
32		10	(a)	Newcastle U	D	1-1	Speedie	36,506
33		16	(h)	Blackburn R	W	2-1	Nevin, Speedie	18,905
34		31	(a)	Cardiff C	D	3-3	Dixon, Lee, Spackman (pen)	11,060
35	Apr	7	(h)	Fulham	W	4-0	Dixon 2, Speedie, Nevin	31,947
36		14	(a)	Crystal Palace	W	1-0	Nevin	20,540
37		21	(h)	Shrewsbury T	W	3-0	Dixon 2, Nevin	18,295
38		24	(a)	Portsmouth	D	2-2	Thomas, Nevin (pen)	19,267
39		28	(h)	Leeds U	W	5-0	Thomas, Dixon 3, Canoville	33,447
40	May	4	(a)	Manchester C	W	2-0	Nevin, Dixon	21,713
41		7	(h)	Barnsley	W	3-1	Speedie, Nevin 2	29,541
42		12	(a)	Grimsby T	W	1-0	Dixon	13,000

FINAL LEAGUE POSITION: 1st in Division Two

Appearances

Sub. Appearances

Goals

Niedzwiecki E	Hollins J	Hutchings C	Pates C	McLaughlin J	Bumstead J	Walker C	Spackman N	Dixon K	Lee C	Canoville P	Speedie D	Jones J	Nevin P	Rhoades-Brown P	McAndrew A	Thomas M	Johnstone D	Jasper D	Dublin K	
1	2	3	4	5	6	7	8	9	10	11										1
1	2	3	4	5	6	7	8	9	10	11										2
1	2	3	4	5	6	7*	8	9	10	11	12									3
1.	2		4	5	6	7	8	9	10	11		3								4
1	2		4	5	6	7	8	9	10		12	3	11*							5
1	2		4	5	6	7	8	9	10*		12	3	11							6
1	2		4	5	6		8	9	10	7		3	11							7
1	2		4	5	6		8	9	10	11	12	3	7*							8
1	2		4	5	6		7	9	10	8		3	11							9
1	2		4	5	6		8	9	10*	7	12	3	11							10
1	2		4	5	6		8	9		7	10	3	11							11
1	2		4	5	6		8	9	12	7	10*	3	11							12
1	2		4	5	6		8	9	12		10	3	7	11*						13
1	2	3	4	5	6		8	9			10		7	11						14
1	2		4	5	6*		8	9	12		10	3	7	11						15
1	2		4	5	6		8	9			10	3	7	11						16
1	2		4	5	6		8	9	12		10	3	7	11						17
1	2		4	5	6		8	9	12		10	3	7	11						18
1	2		4	5	6		8	9		11	10	3	7							19
1	2		4	5	6		8	9		11	10	3	7							20
1	2		4	5	6		8	9	12	11	10*	3	7							21
1	2		4	5	6			9		11	10	3	7		8					22
1	2		4	5	6*			9	12	11	10	3	7		8					23
1	2		4	5			8	9		11	10	3	7		6					24
1	2		4	5			8	9	12	11*	10	3	7		6					25
1			4	5			8	9	2		10	3	7		6	11				26
1			4	5			8	9	2		10	3	7		6	11				27
1			4	5			8	9	2		10	3	7		6	11				28
1			4	5			8	9	2		10	3	7		6	11				29
1	3		4	5			8	9	2		10		7		6*	11	12			30
1	3		4	5			8	9	2		10		7		6	11				31
1			4	5			8	9	2		10	3	7		6	11				32
1			4	5			8	9	2		10	3	7		6	11*	12			33
1			4		12		8	9	2		10	3	7		6*	11		5		34
1			4	5	6		8	9	2		10	3	7			11				35
1			4	5	6		8	9	2	12	10	3	7			11*				36
1			4	5	6		8	9	2		10	3	7			11				37
1			4	5	6		8	9	2		10	3	7			11				38
1			4	5	6*		8	9	2	12	10	3	7			11				39
1			4	5	6		8	9	2	12	10	3*	7			11				40
1	2		4	5			8	9			10		7			11		6	3	41
1	2		4	5	6		8	9			10		7			11		3		42
42	29	4	42	41	30	6	40	42	25	17	32	34	38	6	13	17		3	1	
					1				8	3	5						2			
	1	1			7	3	3	28	3	6	13	1	14	1	4	4				

41

1984-85

1	Aug	25	(a)	Arsenal	D	1-1	Dixon	45,329
2		27	(h)	Sunderland	W	1-0	Canoville	25,554
3		31	(h)	Everton	L	0-1		17,734
4	Sep	5	(a)	Manchester U	D	1-1	Thomas	48,398
5		8	(a)	Aston Villa	L	2-4	Bumstead 2	21,494
6		15	(h)	West Ham U	W	3-0	Lee, Nevin, Speedie	32,411
7		22	(a)	Luton T	D	0-0		16,066
8		29	(h)	Leicester C	W	3-0	Dixon 2, Nevin	18,521
9	Oct	6	(a)	Norwich C	D	0-0		18,272
10		13	(h)	Watford	L	2-3	Dixon 2	25,340
11		20	(a)	Southampton	L	0-1		20,212
12		27	(h)	Ipswich T	W	2-0	Dixon 2	19,213
13	Nov	3	(h)	Coventry C	W	6-2	Dixon 3, Jones K 2, Speedie	17,306
14		10	(a)	Newcastle U	L	1-2	Dixon	23,723
15		17	(h)	West Brom A	W	3-1	Rougvie, Speedie 2	17,573
16		24	(a)	Tottenham H	D	1-1	Dixon	31,197
17	Dec	1	(h)	Liverpool	W	3-1	Dixon, McLauglin, Speedie	40,972
18		8	(a)	Sheffield W	D	1-1	Davies	29,373
19		15	(h)	Stoke C	D	1-1	Dixon	20,534
20		22	(a)	Everton	W	4-3	Davis 3, Pates	29,887
21		26	(a)	Q.P.R.	D	2-2	Dixon (2 pen)	26,610
22		29	(h)	Manchester U	L	1-3	Davies	42,197
23	Jan	1	(h)	Nottingham F	W	1-0	Thomas	21,552
24		19	(h)	Arsenal	D	1-1	Speedie	34,752
25	Feb	2	(a)	Leicester C	D	1-1	Speedie (pen)	15,657
26		16	(h)	Newcastle U	W	1-0	Wood	21,826
27		23	(a)	Coventry C	L	0-1		11,430
28	Mar	2	(a)	Ipswich T	L	0-2		17,735
29		9	(h)	Southampton	L	0-2		15,202
30		16	(a)	Watford	W	3-1	Dixon, McClelland (og), Speedie	16,136
31		30	(a)	Sunderland	W	2-0	Dixon, Thomas (pen)	13,489
32	Apr	6	(h)	Q.P.R.	W	1-0	Dixon	20,340
33		10	(a)	Nottingham F	L	0-2		14,666
34		13	(a)	West Ham U	D	1-1	Speedie	19,003
35		16	(h)	Aston Villa	W	3-1	Bumstead, Evans (og), Thomas (pen)	13,267
36		20	(a)	West Brom A	W	1-0	Dixon	11,196
37		27	(h)	Tottenham H	D	1-1	Nevin	26,310
38	May	4	(a)	Liverpool	L	3-4	Davies, Dixon, Spackman (pen)	33,733
39		6	(h)	Sheffield W	W	2-1	Dixon 2	17,085
40		8	(h)	Luton T	W	2-0	Dixon, Nevin	13,789
41		11	(a)	Stoke C	W	1-0	Speedie	8,905
42		14	(h)	Norwich C	L	1-2	Thomas	22,882

FINAL LEAGUE POSITION: 6th in Division One

Appearances

Sub. Appearances

Goals

Niedzwiecki E	Lee C	Rougvie D	Pates C	McLaughlin J	Jasper D	Nevin P	Spackman N	Dixon K	Speedie D	Canoville P	Jones J	Thomas M	Bumstead J	Jones K	Wood D	Davies G	Johnstone D	Droy M	Dublin R	Isaac R	Francis S	Howard T	No.
1	2	3	4	5	6	7	8	9	10	11													1
1	2	3	4	5	6	7	8	9	10	11*	12												2
1	2	3	4	5	6*	7	8	9	10	11		12											3
1	2	3	4	5		7	8	9	10	12	11*	6											4
1	2	3	4	5		7	8	9*	10	12	11	6											5
1	2	3	4	5		7	8	9	10		11	6											6
1	2	3	4	5		7	8	9	10		11	6											7
1	2	3	4	5		7	8	9	10		11		6										8
1	2	3	4	5			8	9	10		11	7	6										9
1	2	3	4*	5		7	8	9	10		11	12	6										10
1	2*	3	4	5		7	8	9	10	11		6	12										11
1		3	4	5		7	8*	9	10	11		6	12	2									12
1	2	3	4	5		7	8	9	10	11		6											13
1	2	3	4	5*		7	8	9	10	11		6	12										14
1	2	3	4	5*		7	8	9	10	11		6	12										15
1	2	3	4	5		7	8	9	10	11		6											16
1		3	4	5		7	8	9*	10	11		12	6	2									17
1		3	4	5		7	8			11		12	6*	2	9	10							18
1		3	4	5		7	8	9		11*		6		2	10	12							19
1	12		4	5		7	8	9			3	11	6	2	10*								20
1	4			5		7	8*	9	12		3	11	6	2	10								21
1			4	5		7	8	9	12		3	11	6*	2	10								22
1		3	4	5		7	8	9	10			11		2	6								23
1	12	3	4	5		7*	8	9	10	11		6		2									24
1		3	4	5		7	8	9*	10	12	2	11	6										25
1		3	4		5	7	8	9			2		11*	6	10	12							26
1			4		5	7	8	9	10	12	3		11	6*	2		5						27
1		3			5	7	8	9	10	11	2*	6	4					12					28
1		5	4			7	8	9	10	6*		11	12	2					3				29
1						7	8	9	10		5	11	6	2		4			3				30
1			4			7	8	9			5	10	6	2		11			3				31
1			4	5		7	8	9	10			11	6	2					3				32
			4	5		7	8	9	10			11*	6	2		12			3	1			33
			4	5	11	7	8	9	10		2		6						3		1		34
1			4	5		7	8	9	10			11	6*			12			3			2	35
1		4*		5		7	8	9	10	12		11	6						3			2	36
1			4	5		7	8	9				11	6			10			3			2	37
1			4	5		7	8	9			12	11	6			10			3			2*	38
1	2	3		5		7	8	9	10	12	4	11*	6										39
1	2	3		5		7	8	9	10	12	4	11	6*										40
1	2		4	5		7	8	9	10*	12	3	11	6										41
1	2		4	5		7	8	9	10	12	3	11*	6										42
40	20	27	36	36	7	41	42	41	33	15	14	26	21	17	17	10	1	1	10	1	2	4	
	2								2	9	2	1	4	2	2	2	1	1	1				
		1	1	1		4	1	24	10	1	2	5	3		1	6							

1985-86

1	Aug	17	(a)	Sheffield W	D	1-1	Speedie		26,164
2		20	(h)	Coventry C	W	1-0	Speedie		15,679
3		24	(h)	Birmingham C	W	2-0	Rougvie, Jones		16,534
4		28	(a)	Leicester C	D	0-0			11,248
5		31	(h)	West Brom A	W	3-0	Speedie 2, Spackman (pen)		15,376
6	Sep	4	(a)	Tottenham H	L	1-4	Dixon		23,692
7		7	(a)	Luton T	D	1-1	Dixon		10,720
8		14	(h)	Southampton	W	2-0	Dixon, Canoville		15,711
9		21	(h)	Arsenal	W	2-1	Nevin, Spackman (pen)		33,241
10		28	(a)	Watford	L	1-3	Rougvie		16,035
11	Oct	5	(a)	Manchester C	W	1-0	Dixon		20,104
12		12	(h)	Everton	W	2-1	Dixon, Speedie		27,634
13		19	(a)	Oxford U	L	1-2	Dixon		12,072
14		26	(h)	Manchester U	L	1-2	Mclaughlin		42,485
15	Nov	2	(a)	Ipswich T	W	2-0	Dixon, Speedie		15,324
16		9	(h)	Nottingham F	W	4-2	Speedie, Dixon 2, Hazard (pen)		17,743
17		16	(a)	Newcastle U	W	3-1	Speedie, Spackman, Dixon		22,355
18		23	(h)	Aston Villa	W	2-1	Dixon, Speedie		17,509
19		30	(a)	Liverpool	D	1-1	Nevin		38,482
20	Dec	7	(a)	Coventry C	D	1-1	Murphy		8,721
21		14	(h)	Sheffield W	W	2-1	Speedie, Spackman		19,658
22		21	(a)	Birmingham C	W	2-1	Hagan (og), Nevin		10,594
23		28	(h)	Tottenham H	W	2-0	Dixon, Spackman (pen)		37,115
24	Jan	11	(h)	Luton T	W	1-0	Speedie		21,102
25		18	(a)	West Brom A	W	3-0	Speedie, Murphy, Nevin		10,300
26	Feb	1	(h)	Leicester C	D	2-2	Shearer, Jones		12,372
27		8	(h)	Oxford U	L	1-4	Bumstead		16,181
28	Mar	8	(h)	Manchester C	W	1-0	Reid (og)		17,573
29		16	(a)	Everton	D	1-1	Murphy		30,145
30		19	(h)	Q.P.R.	D	1-1	Nevin		17,871
31		22	(a)	Southampton	W	1-0	Pates		15,509
32		29	(h)	West Ham U	L	0-4			29,955
33		31	(a)	Q.P.R.	L	0-6			18,584
34	Apr	5	(h)	Ipswich T	D	1-1	Speedie		13,072
35		9	(a)	Manchester U	W	2-1	Dixon 2		45,355
36		12	(a)	Nottingham F	D	0-0			18,055
37		15	(a)	West Ham U	W	2-1	Spackman, Nevin		29,361
38		19	(h)	Newcastle U	D	1-1	Nevin		18,970
39		26	(a)	Aston Villa	L	1-3	Spackman (pen)		17,770
40		29	(a)	Arsenal	L	0-2			24,025
41	May	3	(h)	Liverpool	L	0-1			43,900
42		5	(h)	Watford	L	1-5	Speedie		12,017

FINAL LEAGUE POSITION: 6th in Division One

Appearances

Sub. Appearances

Goals

44

Football season appearance/shirt-number grid (shirt number worn by each player per match; `*` denotes substituted).

Niedzwiecki E	Lee C	Rougvie D	Pates C	McLaughlin	Bumstead J	Nevin P	Spackman N	Dixon K	Speedie D	Murphy J	Jones K	Dublin K	Canoville P	Wood P	McAllister K	Davies G	Isaac R	Hazard M	Shearer D	Millar J	Francis S	Godden A	Howard T	Fridge L	Durie G	McNaught J	Match
1	2	3	4	5	6*	7	8	9	10	11	12																1
1	2	3	4	5	6	7		9	10	11	8																2
1	2	3	4	5	6	7		9	10	11	8																3
1	2	3	4	5	6	7	8	9	10	11																	4
1	2	3	4	5	6	7	8	9	10	11																	5
1	2	3	4	5	6	7	8	9	10	11*			12														6
1	2	3	4	5	6	7	8	9	10	11																	7
1		3	4	5	6*	7	8	9					11	2	12	10											8
1		3		5	6	7	12	9					11	2	10		4	8*									9
1		3	4	5	6	7*	11	9	10				12	2				8									10
1		3	4	5	6	7	11	9	10				12	2				8*									11
1		3	4	5	6	7	11	9	10					2				8									12
1		3*	4	5	6	7		9	10	11				2	12			8									13
1		3	4	5	6*	7	8	9	10		12		11	2													14
1			4	5		7	8	9	10			3	11	2													15
1			4	5	6	7	8	9	10		6	3		2				11									16
1			4	5	6	7	8	9	10			3		2				11									17
1			4	5		7	8	9	10			3		2	12			11*									18
1		4		5		7	8	9		11	6	3	12	2	10*												19
1			4	5		7	8	9	10	11*	6	3		2	12												20
1		3	4	5		7*	8	9	10		6		12	2	11												21
1		3	4	5	6*	7	8	9		11			12	2	10												22
1		2	4	5		7	8	9	10	6		3	12		11*												23
1	2	4		5	6	7	8	9	10			3			11												24
1	2		4	5	6	7	8	9	10*	11		3	12														25
1	5	4		6	7	8				12		3		2	10*				11	9							26
1	5	4		6	7	8				10				2					11	9	3						27
1	2*	3	4	5	6			12	9	10	11				8	7											28
1		3	4	5	6	7	8	9	10	11				2													29
1*	12	3	4	5	6	7	8	9	10	11				2													30
		3	4	5	6	7	8	9	10					2	11							1					31
	9	3	4	5	6*	7	8		10					2	11				12			1					32
	2	3	4	5		7*	8	9	10		12				11				6			1					33
			4	5	6	7	8	9	10	11		3										1	2				34
		3	4	5		7	8	9	10	11				2					6			1					35
			4		5	7	8	9	10	11				2					6	3		1					36
			4		5	6*	7	8	9		11			2	12				10	3		1					37
		3*	4	5	6	7	8	9						2	12				10	11		1					38
			4	5	6	12	8	9	10	11				2					7*	3		1					39
		3	4*	5	6	7	8	9	10	11	12			2								1					40
			4		5	7	8	9	10		6		11	2	12				3*			1					41
			4		5		8		10		6		11	2*	7				3					1	9	12	42
30	12	34	35	40	32	39	37	38	34	21	10	11	4	28	13	1	3	17	2	7	3	8	1	1	1		
	1			1	2				4		9			7				1							1		
		2	1	1	1	7	7	14	14	3	2	0	1														

45

1986-87

#	Month	Date		Opponent	Result		Scorers	Attendance
1	Aug	23	(h)	Norwich C	D	0-0		19,887
2		25	(a)	Oxford U	D	1-1	Speedie	11,238
3		30	(a)	Sheffield W	L	0-2		25,853
4	Sep	2	(h)	Coventry C	D	0-0		11,839
5		6	(h)	Luton T	L	1-3	Dixon	13,040
6		13	(a)	Tottenham H	W	3-1	Harzard 2 (1 pen), Dixon	28,202
7		20	(h)	Nottingham F	L	2-6	Nevin, Bumstead	20,171
8		28	(a)	Manchester U	W	1-0	Dixon	33,340
9	Oct	4	(h)	Charlton Ath	L	0-1		15,243
10		11	(a)	West Ham U	L	3-5	Jones (pen), Dixon, Bumstead	26,859
11		18	(h)	Manchester C	W	2-1	Hazard, Bumstead	12,990
12		25	(a)	Arsenal	L	1-3	Bumstead	32,990
13	Nov	1	(h)	Watford	D	0-0		13,334
14		8	(a)	Everton	D	2-2	Jones, Pates	29,727
15		15	(a)	Aston Villa	D	0-0		17,739
16		22	(h)	Newcastle U	L	1-3	Durie	14,544
17		29	(a)	Leicester C	D	2-2	Speedie, Bumstead	10,047
18	Dec	6	(h)	Wimbledon	L	0-4		15,446
19		14	(a)	Liverpool	L	0-3		25,856
20		20	(h)	Tottenham H	L	0-2		21,576
21		26	(a)	Southampton	W	2-1	McLaughlin, Bumstead	12,709
22		27	(h)	Aston Villa	W	4-1	Spackman (pen), Dixon 2, Pates	14,637
23	Jan	1	(h)	Q.P.R.	W	3-1	McNaught 2, Wegerle	20,982
24		3	(a)	Luton T	L	0-1		10,556
25		24	(a)	Norwich C	D	2-2	Bumstead, Wicks	16,562
26	Feb	7	(h)	Sheffield W	W	2-0	Hazard (pen), Madden (og)	12,493
27		10	(h)	Oxford U	W	4-0	Hazard(pen), Durie, Dixon, Nevin	9,546
28		14	(a)	Coventry C	L	0-3		12,906
29		21	(h)	Manchester U	D	1-1	Harzard	26,515
30		28	(a)	Nottingham F	W	1-0	Nevin	18,317
31	Mar	7	(h)	Arsenal	W	1-0	West	29,301
32		14	(a)	Manchester C	W	2-1	McLaughlin, Durie	19,819
33		21	(h)	West Ham U	W	1-0	Nevin	25,386
34	Apr	4	(h)	Everton	L	1-2	Dixon	21,914
35		7	(a)	Charlton Ath	D	0-0		11,530
36		14	(a)	Watford	L	1-3	Jones	14,103
37		18	(a)	Q.P.R.	D	1-1	Coady	18,081
38		20	(h)	Southampton	D	1-1	Nevin	11,512
39		25	(a)	Newcastle U	L	0-1		21,962
40	May	2	(h)	Leicester C	W	3-1	Dixon 2, Durie	11,975
41		5	(a)	Wimbledon	L	1-2	Wegerle	9,572
42		9	(h)	Liverpool	D	3-3	Durie, Bumstead, Speedie	29,245

FINAL LEAGUE POSITION: 14th in Division One

Appearances

Sub. Appearances

Goals

46

Godden A	Wood D	Pates C	Bumstead J	McLaughlin J	Wicks J	Durie G	Spackman N	Dixon K	Speedie D	Murphy J	Nevin P	Millar J	Hazard M	Howard T	Jones K	Rougvie D	McNaught J	McAllister K	Lee C	Dublin K	Isaac R	Wegerle R	Niedzwiecki E	Clarke S	Dodds W	West C	Freestone R	Coady J	#
1	2	3	4	5	6	7	8	9	10	11																			1
1	2	3	4	5	6	7*	8	9	10	11	12																		2
1	2	3	4	5	6	7	8	9	10	11																			3
1	2	6	4	5			8	9	10	11	7	3																	4
1	2	6	4*	5		12	8	9	10	11	7	3																	5
1	2	4		5		12	8	9	10	11	7	3	6*																6
1		4	8	5		12		9	10		7	3	6	2	11*														7
1	2	4	8	5			6	9	10*		7				12	3	11												8
1	2	4	8*	5			6	9	10		7					3	11	12											9
1	2	4	6		5			9			7				8	3	11	10											10
1	2	4	6	5				9			7	12			8	3	11*	10											11
1	2	4*	6	5				9		11	7				8	3		10	12										12
1	11		6	5	4			9			7				8	2		10		3									13
	11	6		5				9			7				8*	2		10		3	4	12							14
	11	6		5		12		9			7*				8	2		10		3	4		1						15
	11	6		5		10		9			7				8*	2				3	4	12	1						16
	12	6	11	5			8	9	10*		7					2				3	4		1						17
	12		6		5		8	9	10		7		11			2				3	4*		1						18
	12	4	6	5		9	8		10	11						2	7*			3			1						19
	2	4	6	5			8	9	10		7							11*		3		12	1						20
	2	4	6	5			8	9	10		7									3		11	1						21
	2	4	6	5*		12	8	9	10		7									3		11	1						22
	2	4		5		12	8	9	10		7						6			3		11*	1						23
	2	4		5		12	8	9	10		7						6			3		11*	1						24
1	2	4	6		5	9	8		10*		7		11							3				12					25
1	2*	8	6		5	9	11		10		7		12							3				4					26
1	12	4	6		5	9*	8		10		7		11							3				2					27
1	12	4	6*		5	9			10		7		8				11			3				2					28
1	12	4		5		9	8		10	11	7		6*							3				2					29
1	12	4	6	5		9*			10	11	7		8							3				2					30
1	6	4		5							7				8				9*	3		11		2	12	10			31
1	6	4		5		9					7		8							3		11		2		10			32
1	6			5	4	9			12		7		8					11		3				2		10*			33
1	6	4		5		9			10		7		8					11		3				2					34
1	6			5	4	9					7		8					11		3		12		2		10*			35
1	2	6*	5			9					7		8					11		3		12		4		10			36
	2		6	5		9					7		8		10					3				4			1	11	37
	6	4		5		10		9			7		8*					11		3				2		12	1	3	38
	11	4	6	5		10		9			7		8*							3				2		12	1	12	39
	8		6	5	4	10		9			7*							11						2		12	1	3	40
	8		6	5	4			9	10				2							3*	7						1	11	41
	2		6	5	4	7		9	10	8										3							1	11	42
26	34	33	29	36	15	18	20	35	22	1	36	4	16	1	16	13	8	7	1	28	5	7	10	15	5	6	5		
	7				7			1			1		2		1			1	1		5	1	1	2			1		
		2	8	2	1	5		10	3		5		6		3		2			2				1		1	1		

47

1987-88

1	Aug	15	(h)	Sheffield W	W	2-1	Dixon, Durie (pen)	21,929
2		18	(a)	Portsmouth	W	3-0	Nevin, Dixon, Wilson C	16,917
3		22	(a)	Tottenham H	L	0-1		37,07-
4		29	(h)	Luton T	W	3-0	Coady, Nevin, Dixon	16,075
5		31	(a)	Manchester U	L	1-3	Walsh (og)	46,478
6	Sep	5	(h)	Nottingham F	W	4-3	Durie 2, Wilson C, Clarke	18,414
7		12	(a)	Queen's Park R	L	1-3	Durie	22,583
8		19	(h)	Norwich C	W	1-0	Dixon	15,242
9		26	(a)	Watford	W	3-0	Durie 2 (1 pen), Dixon	16,213
10	Oct	3	(h)	Newcastle U	D	2-2	McCreedy (og), Dixon	22,071
11		10	(a)	Everton	L	1-4	Dixon	31,004
12		17	(h)	Coventry C	W	1-0	Dixon	16,699
13		24	(a)	Southampton	L	0-3		11,890
14		31	(h)	Oxford U	W	2-1	Wegerle, Nevin	15,027
15	Nov	3	(a)	Arsenal	L	1-3	Nevin	40,230
16		22	(a)	Derby Co	L	0-2		18,644
17		28	(h)	Wimbledon	D	1-1	Durie (pen)	15,608
18	Dec	6	(a)	Liverpool	L	1-2	Durie (pen)	31,211
19		12	(h)	West Ham U	D	1-1	Wilson K	22,450
20		20	(a)	Charlton A	D	2-2	Bodley, Wood (pen)	10,893
21		26	(h)	Queen's Park R	D	1-1	McLaughlin	18,020
22		28	(a)	Norwich C	L	0-3		19,668
23	Jan	1	(a)	Luton T	L	0-3		8,018
24		2	(h)	Tottenham H	D	0-0		29,347
25		16	(a)	Sheffield W	L	0-3		19,859
26		23	(h)	Portsmouth	D	0-0		15,856
27	Feb	6	(a)	Nottingham F	L	2-3	Dixon, Wilson K	18,203
28		13	(h)	Manchester U	L	1-2	West	25,014
29		27	(a)	Newcastle U	L	1-3	Wilson K	17,858
30	Mar	5	(a)	Coventry C	D	3-3	Wilson K 2, Nevin	16,816
31		12	(h)	Everton	D	0-0		17,390
32		19	(a)	Oxford U	D	4-4	Nevin, Bumstead, Dixon 2	8,468
33		26	(h)	Southampton	L	0-1		15,380
34		29	(h)	Watford	D	1-1	West	11,240
35	Apr	2	(h)	Arsenal	D	1-1	Harzard	26,084
36		9	(h)	Derby Co	W	1-0	Harzard	16,996
37		23	(a)	Wimbledon	D	2-2	Durie 2 (1 pen)	15,128
38		30	(h)	Liverpool	D	1-1	Durie (pen)	35,625
39	May	2	(a)	West Ham U	L	1-4	West	28,521
40		7	(h)	Charlton A	D	1-1	Durie (pen)	33,701

FINAL LEAGUE POSITION: 18th in Division One

Appearances

Sub. Appearances

Goals

Niedzwiecki E	Clarke S	Dorigo A	Wisks S	McLaughlin J	Wood D	Nevin P	Harzard M	Dixon K	Durie G	Wilson C	Wilson K	Coady J	McNaught	West C	Bodley M	Pates C	Wgerle R	Freestone R	Hall G	Murphy J	McAllister R	Bumstead J	Digweed P	Hitchcock K	
1	2	3	4	5	6	7	8*	9	10	11	12														1
1	2	3	4	5	6	7	8	9	10	11															2
1	2	3	4	5	6	7	8	9	10*	11	12														3
1	2	3	4	5	6	7		9	10	8		11													4
1		3	4	5	2	7		9	10	8	12	11*	6												5
1	2	3	4	5	6	7	8	9*	10	11	12														6
1	2	3	4	5	6	7	8		10	11	9														7
1	2*	3		5	6	7	8†	9		11	10	14		12		4									8
1	2	3		5	6	7	8*	9	10	11		12				4									9
1	2	3		5	6	7	8	9	10	11						4									10
1	2	3		5	6	7*	8†	9	10	11	12	14				4									11
1	2	3		5	6	7	8	9*		11	10			12		4									12
1	2	3		5	6	7	8		10	11	9					4									13
1*	2	3		5	6	7			10	11	9	12				4	8								14
	2	3		5	6	7			10	11	12	9				4	8*	1							15
	2	3		5	6	7	8*		10	11	12	9†				4	14	1							16
	2*	3		5	6	7		9	10	11						4		1	12	8					17
	2	3		5	6	7		9	10	11						4		1		8					18
	2	3		5	6	7*	8	9		11	10					4	12	1							19
		3		5	6	7*		9		11	10	14				4	8†	1	2		12				20
	4	3		5	6	7		9	10	11	8							1	2						21
	4	3*		5	6	7		10		11	9	12					8	1	2						22
	4	3		5	2		8	9	10	11								1			7	6			23
	4	3		5	2		8	9	10	11							12	1			7*	6			24
	4	3		5	2		8	9		11*				10			12	1			7	6			25
	2	3		5	11	12	8	9*		14	10					4		1			7	6†			26
	2	3*		5	10	7		9		12	8					4	11	1				6			27
	2	3		5	10	7		9			8*			12		4	11	1				6			28
	2†	3		5		7	8	9	6		12			10		4	11*	1	14						29
	5	3				7	8	9		10					6	4			2			11	1		30
	2	3	5		6	7	8	9		10						4						11	1		31
	2	3	5		6	7	8*	9		14	10†					4			12			11	1		32
	2	3	5		6	7	8	9		14	10†					4*			12			11		1	33
	2	3	4	5	6	7	8	9						10								11		1	34
	2	3	4	5	6	7	8	9*	10†					12					14			11		1	35
	2	3	4	5	6	7	8	10*		12				9								11		1	36
	6	3	4	5		7	8	9	10										2			11		1	37
	6	3	4	5		7	8	9	10										2			11		1	38
	6	3	4	5		7	8*	9	10					12					2			11		1	39
	2	3	4	5		7		9	10	11*				12	6							8		1	40
14	38	40	17	36	34	36	28	33	26	27	16	4	1	3	6	16	8	15	8	2	4	17	3	8	
							1			4	9	6		6		1	3	5			1				
	1			1	1	6	2	11	12	2	5	1		3	1		1	6			1				

49

1988-89

1	Aug	27	(h)	Blackburn R	L	1-2	Wilson K	8,722
2		30	(a)	Crystal Palace	D	1-1	Wilson K	17,490
3	Sep	3	(a)	Bournemouth	L	0-1		8,763
4		10	(h)	Oxford U	D	1-1	McAllister	7,587
5		17	(a)	Barnsley	D	1-1	Roberts (pen)	6,942
6		20	(h)	Manchester C	L	1-3	Pates	8,858
7		24	(a)	Leeds U	W	2-0	Bumstead, Durie	26,080
8	Oct	1	(h)	Leicester C	W	2-1	Lee, Roberts (pen)	7,050
9		4	(h)	Walsall	W	2-0	Dixon, Durie	6,747
10		9	(a)	Swindon T	D	1-1	Dixon	11,347
11		15	(a)	Oldham A	W	4-1	Wilson K, Nicholas, McAllister, Wood	7,817
12		22	(h)	Plymouth Argyle	W	5-0	Dixon, Durie 2, Roberts (pen), Dorigo	12,658
13		25	(a)	Hull C	L	0-3		6,953
14		29	(h)	Brighton & HA	W	2-0	Wilson K, Dixon	15,406
15	Nov	5	(a)	Watford	W	2-1	Durie, Dixon	17,631
16		12	(h)	Sunderland	D	1-1	Wilson K	19,210
17		19	(a)	Bradford C	D	2-2	Lee, Wilson K	11,442
18		26	(h)	Shrewsbury T	W	2-0	Dorigo, Dixon	11,595
19	Dec	3	(a)	Stoke C	W	3-0	Roberts (pen), Wilson C, McAllister	12,288
20		10	(h)	Portsmouth	D	3-3	Dixon, Durie, Wilson K	20,221
21		16	(a)	Birmingham C	W	4-1	Durie 2, Dixon 2	7,897
22		26	(h)	Ipswich T	W	3-0	Durie, Lee, Dixon	17,621
23		31	(h)	West Brom A	D	1-1	Roberts (pen)	25,906
24	Jan	2	(a)	Oxford U	W	3-2	Dixon 2, Wilson C	11,427
25		14	(h)	Crystal Palace	W	1-0	Dorigo	24,184
26		21	(a)	Blackburn R	D	1-1	Dixon	11,713
27	Feb	4	(a)	Walsall	W	7-0	Durie 5, Wilson K, Roberts (pen)	6,860
28		11	(h)	Swindon T	W	3-2	Durie, Gittens (og), MacLaren (og)	17,829
29		18	(a)	Plymouth Argyle	W	1-0	Dixon	13,180
30		25	(h)	Oldham A	D	2-2	Roberts 2 (1 pen)	13,261
31		29	(h)	Hull C	W	2-1	Dixon, Wilson K	11,407
32	Mar	11	(h)	Watford	D	2-2	Dorigo, Roberts (pen)	22,188
33		15	(a)	Brighton & HA	W	1-0	Wilson K	12,600
34		19	(a)	Manchester C	W	3-2	Dixon, Wilson K, Dorigo	40,070
35		21	(a)	Sunderland	W	2-1	Roberts, Wilson K	14,714
36		25	(h)	Bournemouth	W	2-0	Durie, Roberts (pen)	22,467
37		28	(a)	Ipswich T	W	1-0	Durie	22,950
38	Apr	1	(h)	Barnsley	W	5-3	Dixon 4, Durie	16,023
39		4	(h)	Brimingham C	W	3-1	Wilson K, Roberts, Dixon	14,796
40		8	(a)	West Brom A	W	3-2	Robert (pen), Lee, McAllister	22,858
41		15	(a)	Leicester C	L	0-2		19,468
42		22	(h)	Leeds U	W	1-0	Bumstead	30,332
43		29	(a)	Shrewsbury T	D	1-1	Dixon	5,588
44	May	1	(h)	Stoke C	W	2-1	Dixon, Roberts (pen)	14,946
45		6	(h)	Bradford C	W	3-1	Roberts (pen), Dixon 2	18,003
46		13	(a)	Portsmouth	W	3-2	McAllister 2, Wilson C	12,051

FINAL LEAGUE POSITION: 1st in Division Two

Appearances

Sub. Appearances

Goals

50

#	Hictcock	Clarke	Wilson C	Roberts	McLaughlin	Pates	McAlister	Nicholas	Wilson K	Durie	Bumstead	Wood	Freestone	Hall	Dodds	Dorigo	Dixon	Lee	Beasant	Mitchell	Harzard	Monkou	Le Saux
1	1	2	3	4*	5	6	7	8	9	10	11	12											
2		2	3	4	5			8	9	10	11	6	1	7									
3	1	2	3	4	5	11		8	9	10		6		7*	12								
4		2	3	4	5	11		8	9	10		6	1	7*	12								
5		2	3	4	5		7	8	9	10*	11	6	1	12									
6	1	2	11	4	5		7	8	12	10	6*					3	9						
7		2	6	4	5		7	8	12	10*	11		1			3	9						
8		2		4	5		7	8†		10	11	6*	1	14		3	9	12					
9		2		4	5		7	8		10	11		1			3	9	6					
10				4	5			8		10	11	7	1	2		3	9	6					
11			11	4	5		7	8		10		6	1	2		3	9						
12		2	12	4	5		7*	8	11	10		6	1			3	9						
13		2	12	4	5		7†	8	11	10		6*	1			3	9	14					
14		2	11	4	5		12	8	7	10		6	1			3	9*						
15		2	11	4	5			8	7	10		6	1			3	9*	12					
16		2†	11	4	5		12	8	7	10		6*	1			3	9	14					
17			11	4			12	8	7	10		6*	1	2		3	9	5					
18			11	4				8	7	10		6	1	2		3	9	5					
19			11	4			10	8	7			6	1	2		3	9	5					
20			11	4			12	8	7	10*		6	1	2		3	9	5					
21			11	4				8	7	10		6	1	2		3	9	5					
22			11	4	5		12		7	10	14	6	1	2		3†	9	8*					
23			11	4	5		12		7	10	8*	6	1	2		3	9						
24			11	4	5		12		7	10*	14	6	1	2		3	9	8†					
25		2	11	4*	5		7					6		12		3	9	10	1	8			
26		2	11	4	5		7					6				3	9	10	1	8			
27		2	3	4	5			8	7	10		6							1	9	11		
28		2		4	5			8	7	10		6				3			1	9	11		
29		2		4	5			8	12	10		6				3	9	14	1	7	11*		
30		2		4	5		12	8	7			6				3	9		1	10*	11		
31		2	11	4	5		7	8		10		6				3	9		1				
32		2	11	4	5		7	8		10		6				3	9		1				
33		2	11	4	5		7	8		10		6				3	9		1				
34		2	12	4	5		7	8	11	10*		6				3	9		1				
35		2		4	5		7	8	11	10		6				3	9		1				
36		2		4	5		7	8	11	10		6				3	9		1				
37		2		4	5		7	8	11	10		6				3	9		1				
38		2		4*	5		7	8	11	10		6				3	9	12	1				
39		2		4	5*		7	8	11	10		6				3	9	12	1				
40		2		4			7	8*	11	10		6		12		3	9	5	1				
41		2		4	5		7	8	11	10		6*				3	9	12	1				
42		2		4	5		7	8	11	10		6				3	9		1				
43		2	8	4	5		7		11	10*		6		12		3	9		1				
44		2	8	4	5*		7		11			6		10		3	9		1			12	
45		2	10	4	5		7	8	11			6				3	9		1				
46		2†	11	4	5		7	8		10		6				3	9*		1			12	14
	3	36	29	46	31	10	28	39	43	32	27	21	21	17		40	39	12	22	6	4		
			3				8		3		2	1		5	2			8				2	1
			3	15		1	6	1	13	17	2	1				6	25	4					

1989-90

1	Aug	19	(a)	Wimbledon	W	1-0	Wilson K	14,625
2		22	(h)	Q.P.R.	D	1-1	Dorigo	24,354
3		26	(h)	Sheffield W	W	4-0	Roberts (pen), Harper (og), Dixon, McAllister	16,265
4		29	(a)	Charlton Ath	L	0-3		17,221
5	Sep	9	(h)	Nottingham F	D	2-2	Durie, Dixon	21,523
6		16	(a)	Tottenham H	W	4-1	Dixon, Wilson K 2, Clarke	16,260
7		23	(h)	Coventry C	W	1-0	Wilson K	18,247
8		30	(h)	Arsenal	D	0-0		31,833
9	Oct	14	(a)	Norwich C	L	0-2		19,042
10		21	(a)	Derby Co	W	1-0	Dixon	17,279
11		28	(h)	Manchester C	D	1-1	Dixon	21,917
12	Nov	4	(h)	Millwall	W	4-0	Wilson K 2, Dixon 2	24,969
13		11	(a)	Everton	W	1-0	Clarke	33,737
14		18	(h)	Southampton	D	2-2	Monkou, Wilson K	23,093
15		25	(a)	Manchester U	D	0-0		47,106
16	Dec	2	(h)	Wimbledon	L	2-5	Dixon, Roberts (pen)	19,975
17		9	(a)	Q.P.R.	L	2-4	Dickens, Clarke	17,935
18		16	(h)	Liverpool	L	2-5	Durie, Dixon	31,005
19		26	(a)	Crystal Palace	D	2-2	Dixon, Le Saux	24,680
20		30	(a)	Luton T	W	3-0	Wilson K 2, Dixon	10,068
21	Jan	1	(h)	Aston Villa	L	0-3		23,990
22		14	(a)	Sheffield W	D	1-1	Lee	18,042
23		20	(h)	Charlton Ath	W	3-1	Wilson K 2, Dixon	15,667
24	Feb	3	(a)	Coventry C	L	2-3	Dorigo, Dixon	15,243
25		10	(h)	Tottenham H	L	1-2	Bumstead	28,130
26		17	(a)	Nottingham F	D	1-1	Roberts	22,500
27		24	(h)	Manchester U	W	1-0	Hall	29,979
28	Mar	3	(a)	Southampton	W	3-2	Wilson K, Dorigo, Durie	16,526
29		10	(h)	Norwich C	D	0-0		18,796
30		17	(a)	Arsenal	W	1-0	Bumstead	33,805
31		21	(a)	Manchester C	D	1-1	Durie	24,670
32		31	(h)	Derby Co	D	1-1	Wilson K	14,265
33	Apr	7	(h)	Luton T	W	1-0	Durie	15,221
34		14	(a)	Aston Villa	L	0-1		28,361
35		16	(h)	Crystal Palace	W	3-0	Dixon, Wilson K, Stuart	16,132
36		21	(a)	Liverpool	L	1-4	Dixon	38,431
37		28	(h)	Everton	W	2-1	Dixon 2	13,879
38	May	5	(a)	Millwall	W	3-1	Dixon 3	12,230

FINAL LEAGUE POSITION: 5th in Division One

Appearances

Sub. Appearances

Goals

Beasant	Clarke	Dorigo	Roberts	Lee	Monkou	Dickens	Nicholas	Dixon	Durie	McAllister	Wilson K	Bumstead	Wilson C	Hazard	Johnsen	Le Saux	Hall	Stuart	Matthew	
1	2	3	4	5	6	7	8	9	10†	11*	12	14								1
1	2	3	4	5	6	7	8	9	10	11										2
1	2	3	4	5	6	7	8	9		11	10									3
1	2	3	4	5	6	7	8	9	10†	11*	12	14								4
1	2		4	5	6	7†	8	9*	10		12	14	3	11						5
1	2		4	5	6	7*	8	9			10	12	3	11						6
1	2*	3	4	5	6	7	8	9			10	12		11						7
1	2	3	4*	5	6	7	8	9			10	12		11						8
1	2	3		5	6	7*	8	9		12	10	4	14	11†						9
1	2*	3	4	5	6	7	8	9			10	12		11						10
1	2*	3	4	5	6	7	8	9			10	12		11						11
1	2	3	4	5	6	7	8	9			10			11						12
1	2	3	4	5	6	7	8	9			10			11						13
1	2	3	4	5	6	7	8	9			10			11						14
1	2	3	4	5	6	7	8	9			10			11						15
1		3	4	5	6†	7	8*	9		12	10	2	14	11						16
1	2	3	4	5		7		9		12	10	8	14	11†	6*					17
1	2	3	4	5	6	7		9	10		8		11							18
1	2	3	4	5	6			9		7	10	8*	11			12				19
1	2	3	4	5	6			9		7	10	8	11							20
1	2	3	4	5	6	14		9		7	10	8*	11†			12				21
1	2		4	8	6			9		11	10	7			5	3				22
1	2	3	4*		6		8	9		7	10	12			5	11				23
1	2	3	4	12			8*	9		7	10	6	11		5					24
1	2	3	4				8	9		7	10	6	11		5					25
1		3	4				8	9		7	10	6	11*		5	12	2			26
1		3	12		6		8	9		7	10	4	11		5		2*			27
1		3	12		6	14	8	9		7	10	4	11†		5		2*			28
1		3			6		8	9	10	7	11	4			5		2			29
1		3			6		8	9	10	7	11	4			5		2			30
1		3			6		8	9	10	7	11	4			5		2			31
1		3			6		8	9	10	7	11	4			5		2			32
1		3	12		6		8	9	10	7	11†	4*	14		5		2			33
1		3			6		8	9	10	7	11	4			5		2			34
1		3	12		6		8	9	10†				14		5	11	2	4*	7	35
1		3	12		6		8	9	10	7	11†	4*	14		5		2			36
1		3			6			9	10	7	8	4	11		5		2			37
1		3	12		6	14	8†	9	10						5	11	2*	7	4	38
38	24	35	24	23	34	20	29	38	14	21	33	21	12	13	18	4	13	2	2	
				7		2			1	3	4	8	6			3				
6	3	3	3	1	1	1		20	5	1	14	2				1	1	1		

53

1990-91

1	Aug	25	(h)	Derby Co	W	2-1	Lee, Nicholas	24,652
2		28	(a)	Crystal Palace	L	1-2	Dorigo	27,101
3	Sep	1	(a)	Q.P.R.	L	0-1		19,813
4		8	(h)	Sunderland	W	3-2	Dixon, Wilson, Wise (pen)	19,424
5		15	(a)	Arsenal	L	1-4	Wilson	41,516
6		22	(h)	Manchester C	D	1-1	Wilson	20,924
7		29	(h)	Sheffield U	D	2-2	Wilson 2	19,873
8	Oct	6	(a)	Southampton	D	3-3	Clarke, Wilson, Wise (pen)	16,911
9		20	(h)	Nottingham F	D	0-0		22,403
10		27	(a)	Liverpool	L	0-2		38,463
11	Nov	3	(h)	Aston Villa	W	1-0	Le Saux	23,555
12		10	(h)	Norwich C	D	1-1	Wise (pen)	16,925
13		17	(a)	Wimbledon	L	1-2	Durie	10,773
14		25	(a)	Manchester U	W	3-2	Pallister (og), Townsend, Wise (pen)	37,836
15	Dec	1	(h)	Tottenham H	W	3-2	Dixon, Bumstead, Durie	33,478
16		8	(h)	Crystal Palace	W	2-1	Stuart, Durie	21,558
17		15	(a)	Derby Co	W	6-4	Dixon 2, Durie 2, Wise, Le Saux	15,057
18		22	(h)	Coventry C	W	2-1	Townsend, Wise	16,317
19		26	(a)	Leeds U	L	1-4	Dixon	30,893
20		29	(a)	Luton T	L	0-2		11,050
21	Jan	1	(h)	Everton	L	1-2	Wilson	18,351
22		12	(h)	Q.P.R.	W	2-0	Durie 2	19,255
23		29	(a)	Sunderland	L	0-1		20,038
24	Feb	2	(h)	Arsenal	W	2-1	Stuart, Dixon	29,094
25		9	(a)	Manchester C	L	1-2	Wise	25,116
26		16	(h)	Wimbledon	D	0-0		13,378
27	Mar	2	(a)	Tottenham H	D	1-1	Durie	26,168
28		9	(h)	Manchester U	W	3-2	Durie, Dorigo, Monkou	22,818
29		16	(a)	Sheffield U	L	0-1		20,581
30		23	(h)	Southampton	L	0-2		13,391
31		30	(h)	Leeds U	L	1-2	Le Saux	17,585
32	Apr	1	(a)	Coventry C	L	0-1		14,272
33		6	(h)	Luton T	D	3-3	Le Saux, Stuart, Wise (pen)	12,603
34		13	(a)	Everton	D	2-2	Dixon 2	19,526
35		17	(a)	Norwich C	W	3-1	Wise, Durie 2	12,301
36		20	(a)	Nottingham F	L	0-7		20,305
37	May	4	(h)	Liverpool	W	4-2	Dixon 2, Wise (pen), Durie	32,266
38		11	(a)	Aston Villa	D	2-2	Cundy, Stuart	27,866

FINAL LEAGUE POSITION: 11th in Division One

Appearances

Sub. Appearances

Goals

Beasant	Hall	Dorigo	Townseand	Johnstone	Lee	Wise	Nicholas	Dixon	Wilson	Le Saux	McAlister	Cundy	Bumstead	Monkou	Dickens	Clarke	Durie	Hitchcock	Stuart	Matthew	Mitchell	Sinclair	Myers	Burley	Pearce	No.
1	2	3	4	5	6	7	8	9	10	11*	12															1
1	2	3	4	5	6	7	8	9	10	11*	12															2
1	2	3	4		6	7	8	9	10	11		5														3
1	2	3	4		6	7	8†	9	10	11*	12	5	14													4
1	2	3	4		6		8*	9	10		12	5	11†	4	14											5
1		3	4	5*	12		8	9	10	11	7			6		2										6
1		3	4		5	7	8	9	10	11				6		2										7
1		3	4		5	7	8	9		11		12		6		2	10*									8
1		3	4		5	7	8	9*		11	14	12		6		2	10									9
1		3	4		5	11	8*	9	14	7		12		6		2†	10									10
	2	3	4		5	7		9		11		12	8	6*			10	1								11
	2	3	4		6	7		9		11	12	5	8*				10	1								12
	2	3	4		6	7	8*	9		11	12	5					10	1								13
1	2		4		11			9	12	3		5		6			10*		7	8						14
1	2	3	4		11			9		7		5	8	6			10									15
1	2		4		11			9		3		5	8	6			10		7							16
1	2	3			8	11*	14	9	12	7		5		6†			10		4							17
1	2	3	4		8	11		9		7		5		6*			10		12							18
1	2	3*	4		6	11		9	12	7		5					10		8							19
1	2	6	4*		11			9	10	3	12	5	8†		14				7							20
1	2	6			11			9	10	7*	12	5	8				3		4							21
1	2	3	4					9		11		5		6			10		7	8						22
1	2	3	4		14			9		11†		5	12	6			10		7	8*						23
1	2	3	4		11			9†	14	7*		5	12	6			10		8							24
1	2*	3	4		11			10†		7		5	4*	6	14		12		9	8						25
1		3			11			9		7		5	4*	6	8	2							12	10		26
1		3	4		14	11*		9	12			5		6	8	2	10		7†							27
1		3	4		11			9		7		5		6	8	2	10									28
1		3	4		11			9*		7		5		6	8	2	10		12							29
1		3	4		11			9*				5		6	8	2	10		7	12						30
1		3	4		11			9		7		5		6	8	2	10									31
1		3	4		11			9		7		5		6	8	2	10									32
1	2		4		6	11				7		5	8						9	10*		3	12			33
1	2		4		12	11		9		7		5	8	6					10*			3				34
1	2		4		11			9		7		5		6	8		10					3*	12	14		35
1		11	4		5			9†					8	6			10		7			3*	12	14		36
1		3	4		11			9	12			5		6	8	2	10		7*							37
1		3	4		11			9				5†		6	8*	2	10		7			12		14		38
35	24	31	34	6	17	33	11	33	17	24	5	28	8	27	13	17	24	3	17	6	1	4				
			4		1			5	4	8	1	5	3	1			2	2				3	1	1		
		2	2		1	10	1	10	7	4			1	1		1	12		4							

1991-92

1	Aug	17	(h)	Wimbledon	D	2-2	Elliott, Allon	22,574
2		21	(a)	Olham Ath	L	0-3		14,997
3		24	(a)	Tottenham H	W	3-1	Dixon, Wilson, Townsend	34,645
4		28	(h)	Notts Co	D	2-2	Elliott, Allon	15,847
5		31	(h)	Luton T	W	4-1	Le Saux, Townsend, Dixon, Wise	17,457
6	Sep	3	(a)	Sheffield U	W	1-0	Wise	17,400
7		7	(a)	West Ham U	D	1-1	Dixon	18,875
8		14	(h)	Leeds U	L	0-1		23,439
9		18	(h)	Aston Villa	W	2-0	Jones, Townsend	17,182
10		21	(a)	Q.P.R.	D	2-2	Townsend, Wise	19,579
11		28	(h)	Everton	D	2-2	Wilson, Wise	19,038
12	Oct	5	(a)	Arsenal	L	2-3	Le Saux, Wilson	42,074
13		19	(h)	Liverpool	D	2-2	Jones, Myers	30,230
14		26	(a)	Crystal Palace	D	0-0		21,841
15	Nov	2	(a)	Coventry C	W	1-0	Le Saux	11,343
16		16	(h)	Norwich C	L	0-3		15,755
17		23	(a)	Southampton	L	0-1		14,933
18		30	(h)	Nottingham F	W	1-0	Dixon	19,420
19	Dec	7	(a)	Sheffield W	L	0-3		27,383
20		15	(h)	Manchester U	L	1-3	Allen C	23,120
21		21	(h)	Oldham Ath	W	4-2	Wise (pen), Allen C 2, Elliott	13,136
22		26	(a)	Notts Co	L	0-2		11,933
23		28	(a)	Luton T	L	0-2		10,738
24	Jan	1	(h)	Manchester C	D	1-1	Allen C	18,196
25		11	(h)	Tottenham H	W	2-0	Allen C, Wise	28,628
26		18	(a)	Wimbledon	W	2-1	Townsend, Allen C	8,413
27	Feb	1	(a)	Liverpool	W	2-1	Jones, Wise	38,681
28		8	(h)	Crystal Palace	D	1-1	Cascarino	17,810
29		12	(h)	Southampton	D	1-1	Townsend	7,148
30		22	(a)	Nottingham F	D	1-1	Allen C	24,095
31		26	(a)	Manchester U	D	1-1	Donaghy (og)	44,872
32		29	(h)	Sheffield W	L	0-3		17,538
33	Mar	11	(a)	Norwich C	W	1-0	Dixon	13,413
34		14	(h)	Coventry C	L	0-1		10,962
35		21	(h)	Sheffield U	L	1-2	Cundy	11,247
36		28	(a)	Manchester C	D	0-0		23,633
37	Apr	4	(h)	West Ham U	W	2-1	Wise, Cascarino	20,684
38		11	(a)	Leeds U	L	0-3		31,363
39		18	(h)	Q.P.R.	W	2-1	Clarke, Wise (pen)	18,952
40		20	(a)	Aston Villa	L	1-3	Sinclair	19,269
41		25	(h)	Arsenal	D	1-1	Wise	26,003
42	May	2	(a)	Everton	L	1-2	Newton	20,163

FINAL LEAGUE POSITION: 14th in Division One

Appearances

Sub. Appearances

Goals

Beasant	Clarke	Boyd	Townsend	Elliott	Monkou	Le Saux	Hall	Dixon	Wilson	Wise	Dickens	Allon	Sinclair	Hitchcock	Johnson	Myers	Jones	Matthew	Pearce	Cundy	Stuart	Lee	Allen C	Burnley	Cascarino	Gilkes	Barnard	Newton	
1	2	3	4	5	6	7	8*	9	10†	11	12	14																	1
1	2	3	4	5	6	7		9	12	11	8*	14	10†																2
	2	3	4	5		7		9	10	11	8			1	6														3
	2	3	4	5		7*		9	10	11	8†	12		1	6	14													4
	2	3	8	5	6	7		9	10*	11	12			1			4												5
	2	3	8	5	6	7		9	10	11				1			4												6
	2	3	8	5	6	7		9	10*	11	12			1			4												7
	2	3†	8	5	6	7		9	10*	11	14	12		1			4												8
1	2	3	8	5	6	7		9		11	12	10*					4												9
1	2	3*	8	5	6	7		9	10	11	12						4												10
1	2	3	8	5	6	7		9	10	11							4												11
	2	3*	8	5	6	7		9	10	11	12			1			4												12
	2	3*	8	5	6	7			10			9†		1		11	4	12	14										13
	2	3	8	5		7*		9	10					1			4	12		6		11							14
1	2	3		5		7		9	10	11							4		8	6									15
1	2			5	6	7		9	10	11						3*	4		8†	14		12							16
	2			5	6	7		9	10	11	8	12		1			4					3*							17
	2	3	8	5	6	7		9		11				1			4					10							18
	2	3	8	5	6	7*		9		11†				1			4		12			10	14						19
	2	3*	8	5	6	7		9		11				1			4		12			10							20
1	2		8	5	6	3		9		11							4			7		10							21
1	2	14	8	5	6†	3		9	12	11							4			7*		10							22
1	2*	3	8	5	6	7		9		11	14						4†			12		10							23
1		3	8	5		7*	2	9		11							4		6	12		10							24
			8	5		3	2	9	12	11				1			4†		6	7*		10	14						25
		3	8	5			2	9		11				1			4		6	7		10							26
		3	8			5	7†	2		11				1			4		6	9		10							27
		8	5	3*		7†	2	14†	11					1			4		6	12		10		9					28
		8	5			7		14			4		3	1	6				11*	10	2	9	12						29
			5				2	12	14	11	8			1		3			6	7*		10	4†	9					30
			8	5		7*	2	12	11					1		3	4		6	9		10							31
			8	5		7	2	12	11†					1		3			6	14		10	4	9*					32
1	2		8		6	7		9			3						4		5	11				10					33
1	2		8	5*	6	7		9†	14					3			4			11		12	10						34
1	2		5			12		9*	11				3†		14		4		6	7		10	8						35
1	2				6	7			11					5	3	4			9			8	10						36
1	2			5	6	7			11					3	4*				9			8	10	12					37
1	2†		8	5	6	7*		14	11					3	4				9			10	12						38
1	2		8	5*	6	7		9		11				3			4			10			12						39
1	2†		8		6	7		9		11				3	14		4*	12		10			5						40
1			8		6†	3	14	9		11				2	5		4	12	7*			10							41
1			8		6	3†		9		11				2	5		4	12	7*			10			14				42
21	31	22	35	35	31	39	9	32	15	37	6	2	8	21	6	9	35	2	12	20	1	15	6	11	1				
	1			1	1	3	7	1	4	9		1	2		5	2		7	1	2		1	2		1	3	1		
	1	6	3		3	6	5	3	10		2	1		1	3			1			7		2		1				

1992-93

1	Aug	15	(h)	Oldham A	D 1-1	Harford	20,699
2		19	(a)	Norwich C	L 1-2	Stuart	15,164
3		22	(a)	Sheffield W	D 3-3	Jones, Stuart, Newton	26,338
4		26	(h)	Blackburn R	D 0-0		19,575
5		29	(h)	Q.P.R.	W 1-0	Harford	22,910
6	Sep	2	(a)	Aston Villa	W 3-1	Fleck, Newton, Wise	19,125
7		5	(a)	Liverpool	L 1-2	Harford	34,199
8		12	(h)	Norwich C	L 2-3	Harford, Townsend	16,880
9		20	(a)	Manchester C	W 1-0	Harford	22,420
10		26	(h)	Nottingham F	D 0-0		19,760
11	Oct	3	(a)	Arsenal	L 1-2	Wise	27,780
12		17	(h)	Ipswich T	W 2-1	Hall, Harford	16,707
13		24	(a)	Coventry C	W 2-1	Harford, Stuart	15,626
14		31	(h)	Sheffield U	L 1-2	Towsend	13,763
15	Nov	7	(h)	Crystal Palace	W 3-1	Shaw (og), Stuart, Harford	17,141
16		21	(a)	Everton	W 1-0	Fleck	17,418
17		29	(h)	Leeds U	W 1-0	Townsend	24,345
18	Dec	5	(a)	Tottenham H	W 2-1	Newton 2	31,540
19		11	(a)	Middlesbrough	D 0-0		15,599
20		19	(h)	Manchester U	D 1-1	Lee	34,464
21		26	(h)	Southampton	D 1-1	Newton	18,344
22		28	(a)	Wimbledon	D 0-0		14,687
23	Jan	9	(h)	Manchester C	L 2-4	Stuart, Spencer	15,939
24		16	(a)	Nottingham F	L 0-3		23,249
25		27	(a)	Q.P.R.	D 1-1	Spencer	15,806
26		30	(h)	Sheffield W	L 0-2		16,261
27	Feb	6	(a)	Oldham A	L 1-3	Harford	11,772
28		10	(h)	Liverpool	D 0-0		20,981
29		13	(h)	Aston Villa	L 0-1		20,081
30		21	(a)	Blackburn R	L 0-2		14,780
31	Mar	1	(h)	Arsenal	W 1-0	Stuart	17,725
32		10	(h)	Everton	W 0-2	Stuart, Spencer	12,739
33		15	(a)	Crystal Palace	D 1-1	Stuart	12,610
34		20	(h)	Tottenham H	D 1-1	Cascarino	25,157
35		24	(a)	Leeeds U	D 1-1	Donaghy	28,135
36	Apr	3	(h)	Middlesbrough	W 4-0	Donaghy, Spencer, Stuart, Barnhard	13,043
37		6	(a)	Ipswich T	D 1-1	Spencer	17,444
38		10	(a)	Southampton	L 0-1		15,135
39		12	(h)	Wimbledon	W 4-2	Wise (pen), Hall, Spencer, Shipperley	13,138
40		17	(a)	Manchester U	L 0-3		40,139
41	May	1	(h)	Coventry C	W 2-1	Spencer, Cascarino	14,186
42		8	(a)	Sheffield U	L 2-4	Lee, Townsend	24,850

FINAL LEAGUE POSITION: 11th in Premier Division

Appearances

Sub. Appearances

Goals

Beasant	Clarke	Hall	Jones	Elliott	Donaghy	Stuart	Fleck	Harford	Townsend	Matthew	Newton	Allon	Spencer	Wise	Lee	Pearce	Barnes	Spackman	Hitchcock	Sinclair	Le Saux	Barnard	Burnley	Myers	Johnstone	Kharine	Peyton	Hopkins	Cascarino	Shipperley	Livingstone	#
1	2	3	4	5	6	7	8	9	10	11	12																					1
1	2	3	4	5	6	7		9	10	11	12	8	14																			2
1	2	3	4	5	6	7	8	9	10		11	12																				3
1	2	3	4	5	6	7	8	9	10				11																			4
1	2	3	4	5	6	7	8	9	10				11																			5
1	2	3	4	5	6		8	9	10		7		11	12																		6
1		3	4	5	6		8	9	10		7		11	2	3		10															7
		2			6	12	8	9	4		7			11	5			10	1	3												8
		2			6	12	8	9	4		7		14	11	5			10	1	3												9
		2			6	12	8	9	4		7		14	11	5			10	1	3												10
		2			6	12	8	9	4		7			11	5				1	3	12											11
		2			6	7	8	9	4		10			11	5				1	3	12	11										12
		2			6	7	8	9	4		10				5				1	3	12											13
		2			6	7	8	9	4		10		14	11	5				1	3	12											14
		2			6	7	8	9	4		10			11	5				1	3												15
		2			6	7	8	9	4		10			11	5				1	3												16
		2			6	7	8	9	4		10			11	5				1	3												17
		2			6	7	8		4		10			11	5				1	3	9				12							18
		2			6	7	8		4		10			11	5				1	3	9											19
		2			6	7	8		4	12	10			11	5				1	3	9											20
		2			6	7	8		4		10		14	11	5				1	3	9				12							21
		2			6	7	8		4		10			11	5				1	3					9							22
		2			6	7	8	9	4		10		12		5				1	3		11										23
		2			6	7	12	9	4		10		14						1	3		11		8	5							24
	12	2			6	7		9	4		10		8							3		11			5			1				25
	12	2			6	7		9	4		10		8							3		11			5			1	14			26
		2			6	7	12	9	4		10		8		5				1	3		11			14							27
		2			6	12	8	9	4		10		14		5				1	3		11							7			28
		2			6	12	8	9	4		10		14	11	5				1	3									7			29
		2			14	12	7	9	4		10				5			6	1	3		11							8			30
1	2				6	7	8	9	4	12	10		14							3				5	11							31
1	2				6	7	8	9	4		10		14							3				5	11				12			32
1	2				6	7			4		10		8							3	12			5	11				9			33
1	2				6	7			4		10		8	11						3	12			5					9			34
1	2				6	7			4		10		8	11						3				5					9			35
1	2	14			6	7	12		4		10		8							3	11			5					9			36
1	2	10			6	7			4		10		8	11						3				5					9			37
1	2	10			6	7	9		4		10		8							3	12			5	11					14		38
	2	10			6	7			4				8	11						3	12		1	5					9	14		39
1	2	10			6	7			4				8	11						3	12			5					9	14		40
	2	10							4				8	11	3		6			7				5		1		12	9			41
	2	10					14		4				8	11	12		6			3	7		1	5					9			42
17	18	36	7	7	39	31	28	27	41	3	32	1	13	27	23		2	6	20	32	10	8	1	3	13	5		2	8	2		
	2	1			1	8	3	1		1	2		10		2	1				4	5	2				1		2	1	1	1	
	2	1			2	9	2	9	4		5		7	3	2				1					2	1							

59

1993-94

1	Aug	14	(h)	Blackburn R	L	1-2	Peacock	29,189
2		17	(a)	Wimbledon	D	1-1	Wise	11,263
3		21	(a)	Ipswich T	L	0-1		17,355
4		25	(h)	Q.P.R.	W	2-0	Peacock, Cascarino	20,191
5		28	(h)	Sheffield W	D	1-1	Lee	16,652
6	Sep	1	(a)	Tottenham H	D	1-1	Cascarino	27,567
7		11	(h)	Manchester U	W	1-0	Peacock	37,064
8		18	(a)	Coventry C	D	1-1	Peacock	13,586
9		25	(h)	Liverpool	W	1-0	Shipperley	31,271
10	Oct	2	(a)	West Ham U	L	0-1		18,971
11		16	(h)	Norwich C	L	1-2	Peacock	16,923
12		23	(a)	Aston Villa	L	0-1		29,706
13		30	(h)	Oldham A	L	0-1		15,372
14	Nov	6	(a)	Leeds U	L	1-4	Shipperley	35,050
15		20	(h)	Arsenal	L	0-2		26,839
16		22	(h)	Manchester C	D	0-0		10,128
17		27	(a)	Sheffield U	L	0-1		16,119
18	Dec	5	(a)	Blackburn R	L	0-2		16,756
19		11	(h)	Ipswich T	D	1-1	Peacock	13,208
20		27	(a)	Southampton	L	1-3	Stein	14,221
21		28	(h)	Newcastle U	W	1-0	Stein	23,133
22	Jan	1	(a)	Swindon T	W	3-1	Shpperley, Stein, Wise	16,261
23		3	(h)	Everton	W	4-2	Burley, Stein 2 (1 pen), Shipperley	18,338
24		15	(a)	Norwich C	D	1-1	Stein	19,472
25		22	(h)	Aston Villa	D	1-1	Stein	18,348
26	Feb	5	(a)	Everton	L	2-4	Stein 2 (1 pen)	18,201
27		12	(a)	Oldham A	L	1-2	Spencer	12,002
28		27	(h)	Tottenham H	W	4-3	Donaghy, Stein 2 (1 pen), Spencer	19,398
29	Mar	5	(a)	Manchester U	W	1-0	Peacock	44,745
30		16	(h)	Wimbledon	W	2-0	Fashanu (og), Burley	11,903
31		19	(a)	Liverpool	L	1-2	Burley	38,629
32		26	(h)	West Ham U	W	2-0	Bernard, Hoddle	19,545
33		30	(a)	Sheffield W	L	1-3	Spencer	20,433
34	Apr	2	(h)	Southampton	W	2-0	Spencer, Johnson	19,801
35		4	(a)	Newcastle U	D	0-0		32,218
36		13	(a)	Q.P.R.	D	1-1	Wise	15,735
37		16	(a)	Arsenal	L	0-1		34,314
38		23	(h)	Leeds U	D	1-1	Spencer	18,544
39		27	(h)	Swindon T	W	2-0	Wise (pen), Peacock	11,180
40		30	(a)	Manchester C	D	2-2	Fleck, Cascarino	33,594
41	May	4	(h)	Coventry C	L	1-2	Cascarino	8,923
42		7	(h)	Sheffield U	W	3-2	Kjeldbjerg, Stein 2	21,782

FINAL lEAGUE POSITION: 14th in F.A. Premiership

Appearances

Sub. Appearances

Goals

60

Kharine	Clarke	Sinclair	Dow	Johnsen	Donaghy	Hoddle	Spencer	Cascarino	Peacock	Wise	Fleck	Lee	Myers	Kjeldbjerg	Newton	Shipperley	Hall	Hopkin	Hitchcock	Barnard	Stein	Burnley	Spackman	Duberry	#
1	2	3	4†	5	6	7	8	9	10	11	12	14													1
1	2	3			6	7	12	9	10	11	8			5	4										2
1	2		5	6*	7			9	10	11	8†	12	3	4	14										3
1	2		5	6	7			9	10	11				4	3	8									4
1	2		5	6	7			9†	10	11	12	3*		4	8	14									5
1	2	3	5		6*	7		9†	10	11	12			4	8	14									6
1	2	3	5†		6	7		9	10	11				4	8	12	14								7
1	2	3	5		6	7	12		10	11				4	8	9*									8
1	2	3	5		6*	7			10	11				4	8	9	12								9
1	2†	3	5*		6	7	12		10	11				4	8	9	14								10
1	2	3	5			7		10*	8		12			4	11	9		6							11
1	2	3	5	14	6†	7	12				8*			4	11	9	10								12
	2	3			6†	5			10	11				4	8	12	14		1	7*	9				13
		3		6	14	5			10	11	8*			4	7	12		2†	1		9				14
1	2	3	5†	6*			8			11			4	12	10	14				7	9				15
1	2	3			6		8			11			4	7	10			5	9						16
1	2	3			6†		12	8		11			4	5	10*		7			9	14				17
1		3		5	6		12	8		11			7	10*	2	4			9	14					18
1		3		5	6		10	8		11			7		2	4		9	12						19
1	2	6					10			11			4	8	12	3	7	9	5						20
1	2	3	4	5			12	8†		11			7	10*			9	6	14						21
1	2	3	4	5			12	8†		11			7	10*			9	6	14						22
1	2	3	4	5				8		11			7	10			9	6							23
1	2	3	12	5				8			4		7*	10			9	11	6						24
1	2	3	4†	5	14		12		8				10*		7		9	11	6						25
1	2*	3		5	6			8			12	10	7†			14	9	11	4						26
1	2	3		5		7		10		6		8		12		4	9	11							27
1	2		5	3	7		10	11			4	8		12			9	6*							28
1	2	3		5		7		10	11			4	8		12		9*	6							29
1	2	3		5		12		10	11			4	8	9	7*		6								30
1	2	3*	5		7		10	11			4	8	9		12		6								31
1	2		5	14	12	7		10	11			4	8	9†			3	6*							32
1	2	5			6	7†	9	10	11			4		12			3	8							33
1	2	3		5		9†	12	10	11			4	8	7*		14	6								34
1	2	3		5	6	9	10		11			4		12		7	8								35
1	2	3		5		9	10*	8		11			4	7		12	6								36
1	2	3			6	9		10	11	5		4	8		7										37
1	2	3			6	9		10	11	8		4	7		5						12				38
1	2	3	5			9*		10	11	8		4	7				6	12							39
1	2		5	3		9	10*	11	8		4			12			6	7							40
1	2	3	5	12		9		10			8		7*	6		11		4							41
1	2	3	5		12	7		10	11			4	8			9	6*								42
40	39	35	13	27	24	16	13	16	37	35	7	3	6	29	33	18	4	12	2	9	18	20	5	1	
			1	1	4	3	6	4				2	4			3	6	3		9		3	3	4	
			1	1	1	5	4	8	4	1	1		1		4	1	13	3							

61

1994-95

1	Aug	20	(h)	Norwich C	W	2-0	Sinclair, Furlong	23,098
2		27	(a)	Leeds U	W	3-2	Wise (pen), Spencer 2	32,212
3		31	(h)	Manchester C	W	3-0	Peacock, Wise, Vonk (og)	21,740
4	Sep	10	(a)	Newcastle U	L	2-4	Peacock, Furlong	34,435
5		18	(h)	Blackburn R	L	1-2	Speacer	17,513
6		24	(a)	Crystal Palace	W	1-0	Furlong	16,064
7	Oct	2	(h)	West Ham U	L	1-2	Furlong	18,696
8		8	(h)	Leicester C	W	4-0	Spencer 2, Peacock, Shipperley	18,397
9		15	(a)	Arsenal	L	1-3	Wise	38,234
10		23	(h)	Ipswich T	W	2-0	Wise, Shipperley	15,068
11		29	(a)	Sheffield W	D	1-1	Wise	25,356
12	Nov	6	(h)	Coventry C	D	2-2	Spencer, Kjeldbjerg	17,090
13		9	(a)	Liverpool	L	1-3	Spencer	32,855
14		19	(a)	Nottingham F	W	1-0	Spencer	22,092
15		23	(a)	Tottenham H	D	0-0		27,037
16		26	(h)	Everton	L	0-1		28,115
17	Dec	3	(a)	Southampton	W	1-0	Furlong	14,404
18		10	(a)	Norwich C	L	0-3		18,246
19		18	(h)	Liverpool	D	0-0		27,050
20		26	(h)	Manchester U	L	2-3	Spencer (pen), Newton	31,139
21		28	(a)	Aston Villa	L	0-3		32,901
22		31	(h)	Wimbledon	D	1-1	Furlong	16,009
23	Jan	14	(h)	Sheffield W	D	1-1	Spencer	17,285
24		21	(a)	Ipswich T	D	2-2	Stein, Burley	17,619
25		25	(h)	Nottingham F	L	0-2		17,890
26	Feb	4	(a)	Coventry C	D	2-2	Stein, Spencer (pen)	13,423
27		11	(h)	Tottenham H	D	1-1	Wise	30,812
28		25	(a)	West Ham U	W	2-1	Burley, Stein	21,500
29	Mar	5	(h)	Crystal Palace	D	0-0		14,130
30		8	(a)	Manchester C	W	2-1	Stein 2	21,880
31		11	(h)	Leeds U	L	0-3		20,174
32		18	(a)	Blackburn R	L	1-2	Stein	25,490
33		22	(a)	Q.P.R.	L	0-1		15,103
34	Apr	1	(h)	Newcastle U	D	1-1	Peacock	22,987
35		10	(a)	Wimbledon	D	1-1	Sinclair	7,022
36		12	(h)	Southampton	L	0-2		16,739
37		15	(h)	Aston Villa	W	1-0	Stein	17,015
38		17	(a)	Manchester U	D	0-0		42,728
39		29	(h)	Q.P.R.	W	1-0	Sinclair	21,704
40	May	3	(a)	Everton	D	3-3	Furlong 2, Hopkin	33,180
41		6	(a)	Leicester C	D	1-1	Furlong	18,140
42		14	(h)	Arsenal	W	2-1	Furlong, Stein	29,542

FINAL LEAGUE POSITION: 11th in F.A. Carling Premiership

Appearances

Sub. Appearances

Goals

Kharine	Clarke	Sinclair	Kjeldbjerg	Johnsen	Spackman	Rocastle	Shipperley	Furlong	Peacock	Wise	Newton	Hoddle	Spencer	Barnes	Lee	Hall	Hopkin	Myers	Hitchcock	Burley	Minto	Stein	Rix	
1	2	3	4	5	6	7	8	9	10	11	12	14												1
1	2	3	4	5	6	7		9	10	11	12		8											2
1	2	3	4	5	6	7		9	10	11	12		8											3
1	2	3	4	5	6	7		9	10	11	12	14	8											4
1	2	3	4	5	6	7		9	10	11	12		8											5
1	2	3	4	5	6	7		9	10		11		8											6
1	2	3	4	5		7	12	9	10		6		8	11	14									7
1	2	3	4	5	6	7	14	9	10	11	12		8											8
1	2	3	4	5	6	7	12	9	10	11			8											9
1			4	5		7	8	9	10	11	6		3	12	2	14								10
1			4	5	6	7		9		11	8		3		2	10	12							11
			4	5	6	7		9		11	8		2		10	3	1	12						12
			4	5	6	7		9		11	10		8	2	12	3	1	14						13
1			4	5	6	7	12		10	11	9		8	2						14	3			14
1	5	4			6	7		9		11	10		8	2	14					12	3			15
1	5	4			6			12	10	11	9	14	8	2						7	3			16
1	5	4			6			12	10	11	9		8	2	14					7	3			17
1			4	5	6			9	10	11	7		8	2						12	3			18
1			4	5	6	7		9	10	11	2		8	12							3	14		19
1	2		4	5	6			9	10	12	7		8				3			11		14		20
1	2	6		5	11			9	10		8						3			4	12			21
1	2	3	4	5	6			8	10	11	12		7									9		22
1	2	6	4	5	11			8	10	12	7										3	9		23
1		6	4	5	11			8	10	2	7		12			14					3	9		24
1			4	5	6			9	10	12	11		7		2						3	9		25
1	2	6		5	8		12	14	10	11	7									4	3	9		26
1	2	6			7		12		10	11	4	14	8		5						3	9		27
1	2			5	7		12		10		6		8		4				15	11	3	9		28
	2	6		5	4		12		10		7		8					3	1	11		9		29
	2	6		5		7		8	10		4						12	3	1	11		9		30
	2	6		5		7		8	10		4		14				12	3	1	11		9		31
	2	6	4	5	7			8	10						12	14		3	1	11		9		32
	2			5	6	7		8	10		12					4		3	1	11		9		33
	2	6	4	5	11			8	10		7					14			1	12	3	9		34
	6	4		5				8	10		12				2		11		1	7	3	9		35
1	2	6	4	5			12		10				8	14				11		7	3	9		36
1	2	3	4	5	11	7		8	10				12		6	14						9		37
	2	6		5	11	7		8	10				12			4	3		1	14		9		38
1	2	6		5	11	7		8	10				12			4			14		3	9		39
1	2	6		5				8	10				12			4	7			11	3	9		40
	2	6		5				8	10				12			4	7		1	11	3	9		41
1	2	6		5				8	10		7					4		11		12	3	9	14	42
31	29	35	23	33	36	26	6	30	38	18	22	3	26	10	9	4	7	9	11	16	19	21		
							2	4	6		8		3	2					1	9	3			
		3	1			2	10	4	6	1		11			1					2	8			

63

1995-96

1	Aug	19	(h)	Everton	D	0-0		30,189
2		23	(a)	Nottingham F	D	0-0		27,007
3		26	(a)	Middlesbrough	L	0-2		28,826
4		30	(h)	Coventry City	D	2-2	Wise (pen), Hughes	22,718
5	Sep	11	(a)	West Ham U	W	3-1	Wise, Spencer 2	19,228
6		16	(h)	Southampton	W	3-0	Sinclair, Gullit, Hughes	26,237
7		24	(a)	Newcastle U	L	0-2		36,225
8		30	(h)	Arsenal	W	1-0	Hughes	31,048
9	Oct	14	(a)	Aston Villa	W	1-0	Wise	34,922
10		21	(h)	Manchester U	L	1-4	Hughes	30,192
11		28	(a)	Blackburn R	L	0-3		27,733
12	Nov	4	(h)	Sheffield W	D	0-0		23,216
13		18	(a)	Leeds U	L	0-1		36,133
14		22	(h)	Bolton W	W	3-2	Lee, Hall, Newton	17,495
15		25	(h)	Tottenham H	D	0-0		31,059
16	Dec	2	(a)	Manchester U	D	1-1	Wise	42,019
17		9	(h)	Newcastle U	W	1-0	Petrescu	31,098
18		16	(a)	Arsenal	D	1-1	Spencer	38,295
19		23	(a)	Manchester C	W	1-0	Peacock	28,668
20		26	(h)	Wimbledon	L	1-2	Petrescu	21,906
21		30	(h)	Liverpool	D	2-2	Spencer 2	31,137
22	Jan	2	(a)	Q.P.R.	W	2-1	Brazier (og), Furlong	14,904
23		13	(a)	Everton	D	1-1	Spencer	34,968
24		20	(h)	Nottingham F	W	1-0	Spencer	24,482
25	Feb	4	(h)	Middlesbrough	W	5-0	Peacock 3, Spencer, Furlong	21,060
26		10	(a)	Coventry C	L	0-1		20,629
27		17	(h)	West Ham U	L	1-2	Peacock	25,252
28		24	(a)	Southampton	W	3-2	Wise 2 (1 pen), Gullit	15,226
29	Mar	2	(a)	Wimbledon	D	1-1	Furlong	17,048
30		12	(h)	Manchester C	D	1-1	Gullit	17,078
31		16	(a)	Liverpool	L	0-2		40,820
32		23	(h)	Q.P.R.	D	1-1	Spencer	25,590
33	Apr	6	(h)	Aston Villa	L	1-2	Spencer	23,530
34		8	(a)	Bolton W	L	1-2	Spencer	18,021
35		13	(h)	Leeds U	W	4-1	Hughes 3 (1 pen), Spencer	22,131
36		17	(a)	Sheffield W	D	0-0		25,094
37		27	(a)	Tottenham H	D	1-1	Hughes	32,918
38	May	5	(h)	Blackburn R	L	2-3	Wise, Spencer	28,436

FINAL lEAGUE POSITION: 11th in F.A. Carling Premiership

Appearances

Sub. Appearances

Goals

Kharine	Clarke	Myers	Gullit	Johnsen	Sinclair	Spackman	Hughes	Stein	Peacock	Wise	Spencer	Burley	Lee	Newton	Minto	Furlong	Rocastle	Hall	Petrescu	Duberry	Phelan	Dow	Hitchcock	Morris	#
1	2	3	4	5	6	7	8	9*	10†	11	12	13													1
1	2	3	4	5	6	7	8	9*	10†	11	12	13													2
1	2	3	4	5	6		8	9†	10*	11	12		7	13											3
1	2		4	5	6		8		10	11*	9	12	7		3										4
1	2		4	5	6		8		10*	11	9	12	7		3										5
1	2		4	5	6		8			11	9	10*	7		3	12									6
1	2		4	5	6	7	8	9†	10	11				12	3*	13									7
1		3	4	5	6	7	8		10*	11		2		12		9									8
1		3	4	5			8		10	11		2	6	7		9									9
1	2	3	4	5	6		8		10*	11†	12	13		7		9									10
1		3	4	5	6*		8	12		11		2	12	10		9†	7								11
1			4*	5		7	8	9		11		2	6	10		12		3							12
1		5*					8	9		11		7	6	10		12		3	2	4					13
1		5				12	8	9†		11		7*	6	10		13		3	2	4					14
1		5				7*	8			11	12		6	10		9		3	2	4					15
1		5					8			11	9*	7	6	10		12		3	2	4					16
1		5					8			11		7	6	10		9			2	4	3				17
1	12	5					8			11	9†	7	6	10		13			2	4	3*				18
1	3	5				7	8			11	9		6	10					2	4					19
1	3	5				7	8		10*	11	9		6			12			2	4					20
1	3					7	8			11	12		6	10		9*			2	4		5			21
1	3	5				7*	8			11	9†	13	6	10		12			2	4					22
	5					7	8			11*	9		6	10		12			2	4	3		1		23
	5					7	8†			11	12	13	6	10		9*			2	4	3		1		24
	5					7	8†			11	12		6*	10		9			2	4	3		1	13	25
	5					7	8†			11	12	13	6*	10		9			2	4	3		1		26
	5					7	8*			11	12		6	10		9			2	4	3		1		27
	5					7	8			11	12	13	6	10		9†			2	4*	3		1		28
	6	5*				7	8			11	12			10		9			2	4	3		1		29
	5					7	8		10*	11	9		6			12			2	4	3		1		30
	5					7	8*		10	11	9		6			12			2	4	3		1		31
	5					7	8°			11	12	13	6*	10		9†			2	4	3		1	14	32
	5					7	8			11†	9	13	6	10*	3	12			2	4			1		33
	5					7	8			11	9	13	6	10	3*	12			2†	4			1		34
1		5				7	8			11	9*		6	10	3	12			2	4					35
1		5				7	8			11	9		6	10	3	12			2	4*					36
1		5	4			7	8			11	9*		6	10	3	12			2†					13	37
1		5	4			7	8		10*	11	9		6†	14	3	12			2†					13	38
26	21	20	31	18	12	13	31	7	17	34	23	16	29	21	10	14	1	5	22	22	12	1	12		
	1		4	1	3		1			11	1	5	6	2	3	14			2				1		
		3		1			8	5	7	13			1	1		3			1	2					

65

1971-72 SEASON

FIRST DIVISION

Derby County	42	24	10	8	69	33	58
Leeds United	42	24	9	9	73	31	57
Liverpool	42	24	9	9	64	30	57
Manchester City	42	23	11	8	77	45	57
Arsenal	42	22	8	12	58	40	52
Tottenham Hotspur	42	19	13	10	63	42	51
Chelsea	**42**	**18**	**12**	**12**	**58**	**49**	**48**
Manchester United	42	19	10	13	69	61	48
Wolves	42	18	11	13	65	57	47
Sheffield United	42	17	12	13	61	60	46
Newcastle United	42	15	11	16	49	52	41
Leicester City	42	13	13	16	41	46	39
Ipswich Town	42	11	16	15	39	53	38
West Ham United	42	12	12	18	47	51	36
Everton	42	9	18	15	37	48	36
West Brom. Albion	42	12	11	19	42	54	35
Stoke City	42	10	15	17	39	56	35
Coventry City	42	9	15	18	44	67	33
Southampton	42	12	7	23	52	80	31
Crystal Palace	42	8	13	21	39	65	29
Nottingham Forest	42	8	9	25	47	81	25
Huddersfield Town	42	6	13	23	27	59	25

1972-73 SEASON

FIRST DIVISION

Liverpool	42	25	10	6	72	42	60
Arsenal	42	23	11	8	57	43	57
Leeds United	42	21	11	10	71	45	53
Ipswich Town	42	17	14	11	55	45	48
Wolves	42	18	11	13	66	54	47
West Ham United	42	17	12	13	67	53	46
Derby County	42	19	8	15	56	54	46
Tottenham Hotspur	42	16	13	13	58	48	45
Newcastle United	42	16	13	13	60	51	45
Birmingham City	42	15	12	15	53	54	42
Manchester City	42	15	11	16	57	60	41
Chelsea	**42**	**13**	**14**	**15**	**49**	**51**	**40**
Southampton	42	11	18	13	47	52	40
Sheffield United	42	15	10	17	51	59	40
Stoke City	42	14	10	18	61	56	38
Leicester City	42	10	17	15	40	46	37
Everton	42	13	11	18	41	49	37
Manchester United	42	12	13	17	44	60	37
Coventry City	42	13	9	20	40	55	35
Norwich City	42	11	10	21	36	63	32
Crystal Palace	42	9	12	21	41	58	30
West Brom. Albion	42	9	10	23	38	62	28

1973-74 SEASON

FIRST DIVISION

Leeds United	42	24	14	4	66	31	62
Liverpool	42	22	13	7	52	31	57
Derby County	42	17	14	11	52	42	48
Ipswich Town	42	18	11	13	67	58	47
Stoke City	42	15	16	11	54	42	46
Burnley	42	16	14	12	56	53	46
Everton	42	16	12	14	50	48	44
Q.P.R.	42	13	17	12	56	52	43
Leicester City	42	13	16	13	51	41	42
Arsenal	42	14	14	14	49	51	42
Tottenham Hotspur	42	14	14	14	45	50	42
Wolves	42	13	15	14	49	49	41
Sheffield United	42	14	12	16	44	49	40
Manchester City	42	14	12	16	39	46	40
Newcastle United	42	13	12	17	49	48	38
Coventry City	42	14	10	18	43	54	38
Chelsea	**42**	**12**	**13**	**17**	**56**	**60**	**37**
West Ham United	42	11	15	16	55	60	37
Birmingham City	42	12	13	17	52	64	37
Southampton *	42	11	14	17	47	68	36
Manchester United *	42	10	12	20	38	48	32
Norwich City *	42	7	15	20	37	62	29

* Three clubs relegated

1974-75 SEASON

FIRST DIVISION

Derby County	42	21	11	10	67	49	53
Liverpool	42	20	11	11	60	39	51
Ipswich Town	42	23	5	14	66	44	51
Everton	42	16	18	8	56	42	50
Stoke City	42	17	15	10	64	48	49
Sheffield United	42	18	13	11	58	51	49
Middlesbrough	42	18	12	12	54	40	48
Manchester City	42	18	10	14	54	54	46
Leeds United	42	16	13	13	57	49	45
Burnley	42	17	11	14	68	67	45
Q.P.R.	42	16	10	16	54	54	42
Wolves	42	14	11	17	57	54	39
West Ham United	42	13	13	16	58	59	39
Coventry City	42	12	15	15	51	62	39
Newcastle United	42	15	9	18	59	72	39
Arsenal	42	13	11	18	47	49	37
Birmingham City	42	14	9	19	53	61	37
Leicester City	42	12	12	18	46	60	36
Tottenham Hotspur	42	13	8	21	52	63	34
Luton Town	42	11	11	20	47	65	33
Chelsea	**42**	**9**	**15**	**18**	**42**	**72**	**33**
Carlisle United	42	12	5	25	43	59	29

1975-76 SEASON

SECOND DIVISION

Sunderland	42	24	8	10	67	36	56
Bristol City	42	19	15	8	59	35	53
West Brom. Albion	42	20	13	9	50	33	53
Bolton Wanderers	42	20	12	10	64	38	52
Notts County	42	19	11	12	60	41	49
Southampton	42	21	7	14	66	50	49
Luton Town	42	19	10	13	61	51	48
Nottingham Forest	42	17	12	13	55	40	46
Charlton Athletic	42	15	12	15	61	72	42
Blackpool	42	14	14	14	40	49	42
Chelsea	**42**	**12**	**16**	**14**	**53**	**54**	**40**
Fulham	42	13	14	15	45	47	40
Orient	42	13	14	15	37	39	40
Hull City	42	14	11	17	45	49	39
Blackburn Rovers	42	12	14	16	45	50	38
Plymouth Argyle	42	13	12	17	48	54	38
Oldham Athletic	42	13	12	17	57	68	38
Bristol Rovers	42	11	16	15	38	50	38
Carlisle United	42	12	13	17	45	59	37
Oxford United	42	11	11	20	39	59	33
York City	42	10	8	24	39	71	28
Portsmouth	42	9	7	26	32	61	25

1976-77 SEASON
SECOND DIVISION

Wolves	42	22	13	7	84	45	57
Chelsea	**42**	**21**	**13**	**8**	**73**	**53**	**55**
Nottingham Forest	42	21	10	11	77	43	52
Bolton Wanderers	42	10	11	11	74	54	51
Blackpool	42	17	17	8	58	42	51
Luton Town	42	23	6	15	67	48	48
Charlton Athletic	42	16	16	10	71	58	48
Notts County	42	19	10	13	65	60	48
Southampton	42	17	10	15	72	67	44
Millwall	42	17	13	14	57	53	43
Sheffield United	42	14	12	16	54	63	40
Blackburn Rovers	42	15	9	18	42	54	39
Oldham Athletic	42	14	10	18	52	64	38
Hull City	42	10	17	15	45	53	37
Bristol Rovers	42	12	13	17	53	68	37
Burnley	42	11	14	17	46	64	36
Fulham	42	11	13	18	44	61	35
Cardiff City	42	12	10	20	56	67	34
Orient	42	9	16	17	37	55	34
Carlisle United	42	11	12	19	49	75	34
Plymouth Argyle	42	8	16	18	46	65	32
Hereford United	42	8	15	19	57	78	31

1977-78 SEASON
FIRST DIVISION

Nottingham Forest	42	25	14	3	69	24	64
Liverpool	42	24	9	9	65	34	57
Everton	42	22	11	9	76	45	55
Manchester City	42	20	12	10	74	51	52
Arsenal	42	21	10	11	60	37	52
West Brom. Albion	42	18	14	10	62	53	50
Coventry City	42	18	12	12	75	62	48
Aston Villa	42	18	10	14	57	42	46
Leeds United	42	18	10	14	63	53	46
Manchester United	42	16	10	16	67	63	42
Birmingham City	42	16	9	17	55	60	41
Derby County	42	14	13	15	54	59	41
Norwich City	42	11	18	13	52	66	40
Middlesbrough	42	12	15	15	42	54	39
Wolves	42	12	12	18	51	64	36
Chelsea	**42**	**11**	**14**	**17**	**46**	**69**	**36**
Bristol City	42	11	13	18	49	53	35
Ipswich Town	42	11	13	18	47	61	35
Q.P.R.	42	9	15	18	47	64	33
West Ham United	42	12	8	22	52	69	32
Newcastle United	42	6	10	26	42	78	22
Leicester City	42	5	12	25	26	70	22

1978-79 SEASON
FIRST DIVISION

Liverpool	42	30	8	4	85	16	68
Nottingham Forest	42	21	18	3	61	26	60
West Brom. Albion	42	24	11	7	72	35	59
Everton	42	17	17	8	52	40	51
Leeds United	42	18	14	10	70	52	50
Ipswich Town	42	20	9	13	63	49	49
Arsenal	42	17	14	11	61	48	48
Aston Villa	42	15	16	11	59	49	46
Manchester United	42	15	15	12	60	63	45
Coventry City	42	14	16	12	58	68	44
Tottenham Hotspur	42	13	15	14	48	61	41
Middlesbrough	42	15	10	17	57	50	40
Bristol City	42	15	10	17	47	51	40
Southampton	42	12	16	14	47	53	40
Manchester City	42	13	13	16	58	56	39
Norwich City	42	7	23	12	51	57	37
Bolton Wanderers	42	12	11	19	54	75	35
Wolves	42	13	8	21	44	68	34
Derby County	42	10	11	21	44	71	31
Q.P.R.	42	6	13	23	45	73	25
Birmingham City	42	6	10	26	37	64	22
Chelsea	**42**	**5**	**10**	**27**	**44**	**92**	**20**

1979-80 SEASON
SECOND DIVISION

Leicester City	42	21	13	8	58	38	55
Sunderland	42	21	12	9	69	42	54
Birmingham City	42	21	11	10	58	38	53
Chelsea	**42**	**23**	**7**	**12**	**66**	**52**	**53**
Q.P.R.	42	18	13	11	75	53	49
Luton Town	42	16	17	9	66	45	49
West Ham United	42	20	7	15	54	43	47
Cambridge United	42	14	16	12	61	53	44
Newcastle United	42	15	14	13	53	49	44
Preston North End	42	12	19	11	56	52	43
Oldham Athletic	42	16	11	15	49	53	43
Swansea City	42	17	9	16	48	53	43
Shrewsbury Town	42	18	5	19	60	53	41
Orient	42	12	17	13	48	54	41
Cardiff City	42	16	8	18	41	48	40
Wrexham	42	16	6	20	40	49	38
Notts County	42	11	15	16	51	52	37
Watford	42	12	13	17	39	46	37
Bristol Rovers	42	11	13	18	50	64	35
Fulham	42	11	7	24	42	74	29
Burnley	42	6	15	21	39	73	27
Charlton Athletic	42	6	10	26	39	78	22

1980-81 SEASON
SECOND DIVISION

West Ham United	42	28	10	4	79	29	66
Notts County	42	18	17	7	49	38	53
Swansea City	42	18	14	10	64	44	50
Blackburn Rovers	42	16	18	8	42	29	50
Luton Town	42	18	12	12	61	46	48
Derby County	42	15	15	12	57	52	45
Grimsby Town	42	15	15	12	44	42	45
QPR	42	15	13	14	56	46	43
Watford	42	16	11	15	50	45	43
Sheffield Wednesday	42	17	8	17	53	51	42
Newcastle United	42	14	14	14	30	45	42
Chelsea	**42**	**14**	**12**	**16**	**46**	**41**	**40**
Cambridge United	42	17	6	17	53	65	40
Shrewsbury Town	42	11	17	14	46	47	39
Oldham Athletic	42	12	15	15	39	48	39
Wrexham	42	12	14	16	43	45	38
Orient	42	13	12	17	52	56	38
Bolton Wanderers	42	14	10	18	61	66	38
Cardiff City	42	12	12	18	44	60	36
Preston North End	42	11	14	17	41	62	36
Bristol City	42	7	16	19	29	51	30
Bristol Rovers	42	5	13	24	34	65	23

1981-82 SEASON

SECOND DIVISION

Luton Town	42	25	13	4	86	46	88
Watford	42	23	11	8	76	42	80
Norwich City	42	22	5	15	64	50	71
Sheffield Wednesday	42	20	10	12	55	51	70
QPR	42	21	6	15	65	43	69
Barnsley	42	19	10	13	59	41	67
Rotherham United	42	20	7	15	66	54	67
Leicester City	42	18	12	12	56	48	66
Newcastle United	42	18	8	16	52	50	62
Blackburn Rovers	42	16	11	15	47	43	59
Oldham Athletic	42	15	14	13	50	51	59
Chelsea	**42**	**15**	**12**	**15**	**60**	**60**	**57**
Charlton Athletic	42	13	12	17	50	65	51
Cambridge United	42	13	9	20	48	53	48
Crystal Palace	42	13	9	20	34	45	48
Derby County	42	12	12	18	53	68	48
Grimsby Town	42	11	13	18	53	65	46
Shrewsbury Town	42	11	3	18	37	57	46
Bolton Wanderers	42	13	7	22	39	61	46
Cardiff City	42	12	8	22	45	61	44
Wrexham	42	11	11	20	40	56	44
Orient	42	10	9	23	39	61	39

1982-83 SEASON

SECOND DIVISION

Q.P.R.	42	26	7	9	77	36	85
Wolves	42	20	15	7	68	44	75
Leicester City	42	20	10	12	72	44	70
Fulham *	42	20	9	13	64	47	69
Newcastle United	42	18	13	11	75	53	67
Sheffield Wednesday	42	16	15	11	60	47	63
Oldham Athletic	42	14	19	9	64	47	61
Leeds United	42	13	21	8	51	46	60
Shrewsbury Town	42	15	14	13	48	48	59
Barnsley	42	14	15	13	57	55	57
Blackburn Rovers	42	15	12	15	58	58	57
Cambridge United	42	13	12	17	42	60	51
Derby County *	42	10	19	13	49	58	49
Carlisle United	42	12	12	18	68	70	48
Crystal Palace	42	12	12	18	43	52	48
Middlesbrough	42	11	15	16	46	67	48
Charlton Athletic	42	13	9	20	63	86	48
Chelsea	**42**	**11**	**14**	**17**	**51**	**61**	**47**
Grimsby Town	42	12	11	19	45	70	47
Rotherham United	42	10	15	17	45	68	45
Burnley	42	12	8	22	56	66	44
Bolton Wanderers	42	11	11	20	42	61	44

* Game between Derby and Fulham abandoned after 88 minutes but result allowed to stand at 1-0.

1983-84 SEASON

SECOND DIVISION

Chelsea	**42**	**25**	**13**	**4**	**90**	**40**	**89**
Sheffield Wednesday	42	26	10	6	72	34	89
Newcastle United	42	24	8	10	85	53	80
Manchester City	42	20	10	12	66	48	70
Grimsby Town	42	19	13	10	60	47	70
Blackburn Rovers	42	17	16	9	57	46	67
Carlisle United	42	16	16	10	48	41	64
Shrewsbury Town	42	17	10	15	49	53	61
Brighton & Hove Alb.	42	17	9	16	69	60	60
Leeds United	42	16	12	14	55	56	60
Fulham	42	15	12	15	60	53	57
Huddersfield Town	42	14	15	13	56	49	57
Charlton Athletic	42	16	9	17	53	64	57
Barnsley	42	15	7	20	57	53	52
Cardiff City	42	15	6	21	53	66	51
Portsmouth	42	14	7	21	73	64	49
Middlesbrough	42	12	13	17	41	47	49
Crystal Palace	42	12	11	19	42	52	47
Oldham Athletic	42	13	8	21	47	73	47
Derby County	42	11	9	22	36	72	42
Swansea City	42	7	8	27	36	85	29
Cambridge United	42	4	12	26	28	77	24

1984-85 SEASON

FIRST DIVISION

Everton	42	28	6	8	88	43	90
Liverpool	42	22	11	9	78	35	77
Tottenham Hotspur	42	23	8	11	78	51	77
Manchester United	42	22	10	10	77	47	76
Southampton	42	19	11	12	56	47	68
Chelsea	**42**	**18**	**12**	**12**	**63**	**48**	**66**
Arsenal	42	19	9	14	61	49	66
Sheffield Wednesday	42	17	14	11	58	45	65
Nottingham Forest	42	19	7	16	56	48	64
Aston Villa	42	15	11	16	60	60	56
Watford	42	14	13	15	81	71	55
West Brom	42	16	7	19	58	62	55
Luton Town	42	15	9	18	57	61	54
Newcastle United	42	13	13	16	55	70	52
Leicester City	42	15	6	21	65	73	51
West Ham United	42	13	12	17	51	68	51
Ipswich Town	42	13	11	18	46	57	50
Coventry City	42	15	5	22	47	64	50
QPR	42	13	11	18	53	72	50
Norwich City	42	13	10	19	46	64	49
Sunderland	42	10	10	22	40	62	40
Stoke City	42	3	8	31	24	91	17

1985-86 SEASON

FIRST DIVISION

Liverpool	42	26	10	6	89	37	88
Everton	42	26	8	8	87	41	86
West Ham United	42	26	6	10	74	40	84
Manchester United	42	22	10	10	70	36	76
Sheffield Wednesday	42	21	10	11	63	54	73
Chelsea	**42**	**20**	**11**	**11**	**57**	**56**	**71**
Arsenal	42	20	9	13	49	47	69
Nottingham Forest	42	19	11	12	69	53	68
Luton Town	42	18	12	12	61	44	66
Tottenham Hotspur	42	19	8	15	74	52	65
Newcastle United	42	17	12	13	67	72	63
Watford	42	16	11	15	69	62	59
QPR	42	15	7	20	53	64	52
Southampton	42	12	10	20	51	62	46
Manchester City	42	11	12	19	43	57	45
Aston Villa	42	10	14	18	51	67	44
Coventry City	42	11	10	21	48	71	43
Oxford United	42	10	12	20	62	80	42
Leicester City	42	10	12	20	54	76	42
Ipswich Town	42	11	8	23	32	55	41
Birmingham City	42	8	5	29	30	73	29
West Brom	42	4	12	26	35	89	24

1986-87 SEASON

FIRST DIVISION

Everton	42	26	8	8	76	31	86
Liverpool	42	23	8	11	72	42	77
Tottenham Hotspur	42	21	8	13	68	43	71
Arsenal	42	20	10	12	58	35	70
Norwich City	42	17	17	8	53	51	68
Wimbledon	42	19	9	14	57	50	66
Luton Town	42	18	12	12	47	45	66
Nottingham Forest	42	18	11	13	64	51	65
Watford	42	18	9	15	67	54	63
Coventry City	42	17	12	13	50	45	63
Manchester United	42	14	14	14	52	45	56
Southampton	42	14	10	18	69	68	52
Sheffield Wednesday	42	13	13	16	58	59	52
Chelsea	**42**	**13**	**13**	**16**	**53**	**64**	**52**
West Ham United	42	14	10	18	52	67	52
QPR	42	13	11	18	48	64	50
Newcastle United	42	12	11	19	47	65	47
Oxford United	42	11	13	18	44	69	46
Charlton Athletic	42	11	11	20	45	55	44
Leicester City	42	11	9	22	54	76	42
Manchester City	42	8	15	19	36	57	39
Aston Villa	42	8	12	22	45	79	36

1987-88 SEASON

FIRST DIVISION

Liverpool	40	26	12	2	87	24	90
Manchester United	40	23	12	5	71	38	81
Nottingham Forest	40	20	13	7	67	39	73
Everton	40	19	13	8	53	27	70
QPR	40	19	10	11	48	38	67
Arsenal	40	18	12	10	58	39	66
Wimbledon	40	14	15	11	58	47	57
Newcastle United	40	14	14	12	55	53	56
Luton Town	40	14	11	15	57	58	53
Coventry City	40	13	14	13	46	53	53
Sheffield Wednesday	40	15	8	17	52	66	53
Southampton	40	12	14	14	49	53	50
Tottenham Hotspur	40	12	11	17	38	48	47
Norwich City	40	12	9	19	40	52	45
Derby County	40	10	13	17	35	45	43
West Ham United	40	9	15	16	40	52	42
Charlton Athletic	40	9	15	16	38	52	42
Chelsea	**40**	**9**	**15**	**16**	**50**	**68**	**42**
Portsmouth	40	7	14	19	36	66	35
Watford	40	7	11	22	27	51	32
Oxford United	40	6	13	21	44	80	31

1988-89 SEASON

SECOND DIVISION

Chelsea	**46**	**29**	**12**	**5**	**96**	**50**	**99**
Manchester City	46	23	13	10	77	53	82
Crystal Palace	46	23	12	11	71	49	81
Watford	46	22	12	12	74	48	78
Blackburn Rovers	46	22	11	13	74	59	77
Swindon Town	46	20	16	10	68	53	76
Barnsley	46	20	14	12	66	58	74
Ipswich Town	46	22	7	17	71	61	73
West Brom	46	18	18	10	65	41	72
Leeds United	46	17	16	13	59	50	67
Sunderland	46	16	15	15	60	60	63
Bournemouth	46	18	8	20	53	62	62
Stoke City	46	15	14	17	57	72	59
Bradford City	46	13	17	16	52	59	56
Leicester City	46	13	16	17	56	63	55
Oldham Athletic	46	11	21	14	75	72	54
Oxford United	46	14	12	20	62	70	54
Plymouth Argyle	46	14	12	20	55	66	54
Brighton & Hove Alb.	46	14	9	23	57	66	51
Portsmouth	46	13	12	21	53	62	51
Hull City	46	11	14	21	52	68	47
Shrewsbury Town	46	8	18	20	40	67	42
Birmingham City	46	8	11	27	31	76	35
Walsall	46	5	16	25	41	80	31

1989-90 SEASON

FIRST DIVISION

Liverpool	38	23	10	5	78	37	79
Aston Villa	38	21	7	10	57	38	70
Tottenham Hotspur	38	19	6	13	59	47	63
Arsenal	38	18	8	12	54	38	62
Chelsea	**38**	**16**	**12**	**10**	**58**	**50**	**60**
Everton	38	17	8	13	57	46	59
Southampton	38	15	10	13	71	63	55
Wimbledon	38	13	16	9	47	40	55
Nottingham Forest	38	15	9	14	55	47	54
Norwich City	38	13	14	11	44	42	53
QPR	38	13	11	14	45	44	50
Coventry City	38	14	7	17	39	59	49
Manchester United	38	13	9	16	46	47	48
Manchester City	38	12	12	14	43	52	48
Crystal Palace	38	13	9	16	42	66	48
Derby County	38	13	7	18	43	40	46
Luton Town	38	10	13	15	43	57	43
Sheffield Wednesday	38	11	10	17	35	51	43
Charlton Athletic	38	7	9	22	31	57	30
Millwall	38	5	11	22	39	65	26

1990-91 SEASON

FIRST DIVISION

Arsenal	38	24	13	1	74	18	83
Liverpool	38	23	7	8	77	40	76
Crystal Palace	38	20	9	9	50	41	69
Leeds United	38	19	7	12	65	47	64
Manchester City	38	17	11	10	64	53	62
Manchester United	38	16	12	10	58	45	59
Wimbledon	38	14	14	10	53	46	56
Nottingham Forest	38	14	12	12	65	50	54
Everton	38	13	12	13	50	46	51
Tottenham	38	11	16	11	51	50	49
Chelsea	**38**	**13**	**10**	**15**	**58**	**69**	**49**
QPR	38	12	10	16	44	53	46
Sheffield United	38	13	7	18	36	55	46
Southampton	38	12	9	17	58	69	45
Norwich City	38	13	6	19	41	64	45
Coventry City	38	11	11	16	42	49	44
Aston Villa	38	9	14	15	46	58	41
Luton Town	38	10	7	21	42	61	37
Sunderland	38	8	10	20	38	60	34
Derby County	38	5	9	24	37	75	24

Arsenal 2 points deducted
Manchester United 1 point deducted

1991-92 SEASON

FIRST DIVISION

Leeds United	42	22	16	4	74	37	82
Manchester United	42	21	15	6	63	33	78
Sheffield Wednesday	42	21	12	9	62	49	75
Arsenal	42	19	15	8	81	46	72
Manchester City	42	20	10	12	61	48	70
Liverpool	42	16	16	10	47	40	64
Aston Villa	42	17	9	16	48	44	60
Nottingham Forest	42	16	11	15	60	58	59
Sheffield United	42	16	9	17	65	63	57
Crystal Palace	42	14	15	13	53	61	57
QPR	42	12	18	12	48	47	54
Everton	42	13	14	15	52	51	53
Wimbledon	42	13	14	15	53	53	53
Chelsea	**42**	**13**	**14**	**15**	**50**	**60**	**53**
Tottenham	42	15	7	20	58	63	52
Southampton	42	14	10	18	39	55	52
Oldham Athletic	42	14	9	19	63	67	51
Norwich City	42	11	12	19	47	63	45
Coventry City	42	11	11	20	35	44	44
Luton Town	42	10	12	20	38	71	42
Notts County	42	10	10	22	40	62	40
West Ham United	42	9	11	22	37	59	38

1992-93 SEASON

PREMIER DIVISION

Manchester United	42	24	12	6	67	31	84
Aston Villa	42	21	11	10	57	40	74
Norwich City	42	21	9	12	61	65	72
Blackburn Rovers	42	20	11	11	68	46	71
QPR	42	17	12	13	63	55	63
Liverpool	42	16	11	15	62	55	59
Sheffield Wednesday	42	15	14	13	55	51	59
Tottenham	42	16	11	15	60	66	59
Manchester City	42	15	12	15	56	51	57
Arsenal	42	15	11	16	40	38	56
Chelsea	**42**	**14**	**14**	**14**	**51**	**54**	**56**
Wimbledon	42	14	12	16	56	55	54
Everton	42	15	8	19	53	55	53
Sheffield United	42	14	10	18	54	53	52
Coventry City	42	13	13	16	52	57	52
Ipswich Town	42	12	16	14	50	55	52
Leeds United	42	12	15	15	57	62	51
Southampton	42	13	11	18	54	61	50
Oldham Athletic	42	13	10	19	63	74	49
Crystal Palace	42	11	16	15	48	61	49
Middlesbrough	42	11	11	20	54	75	44
Nottingham Forest	42	10	10	22	41	62	40

1993-94 SEASON

F.A. PREMIERSHIP

Manchester United	42	27	11	4	80	38	92
Blackburn Rovers	42	25	9	8	63	36	84
Newcastle United	42	23	8	11	82	41	77
Arsenal	42	18	17	7	53	28	71
Leeds United	42	18	16	8	65	39	70
Wimbledon	42	18	11	13	56	53	65
Sheffield Wednesday	42	16	16	10	76	54	64
Liverpool	42	17	9	16	59	55	60
QPR	42	16	12	14	62	64	60
Aston Villa	42	15	12	15	46	50	57
Coventry City	42	14	14	14	43	45	56
Norwich City	42	12	17	13	65	61	53
West Ham United	42	13	13	16	47	58	52
Chelsea	**42**	**13**	**12**	**17**	**49**	**53**	**51**
Tottenham Hotspur	42	11	12	19	54	59	45
Manchester City	42	9	18	15	38	49	45
Everton	42	12	8	22	42	63	44
Southampton	42	12	7	23	49	66	43
Ipswich Town	42	9	16	17	35	58	43
Sheffield United	42	8	18	16	42	60	42
Oldham Athletic	42	9	13	20	42	68	40
Swindon Town	42	5	15	22	47	100	30

1994-95 SEASON

F.A. PREMIERSHIP

Blackburn Rovers	42	27	8	7	80	39	89
Manchester United	42	26	10	6	77	28	88
Nottingham Forest	42	22	11	9	72	43	77
Liverpool	42	21	11	10	65	37	74
Leeds United	42	20	13	9	59	38	63
Newcastle United	42	20	12	10	67	47	72
Tottenham Hotspur	42	16	14	12	66	58	62
QPR	42	17	9	16	61	59	60
Wimbledon	42	15	11	16	48	65	56
Southampton	42	12	18	12	61	63	54
Chelsea	**42**	**13**	**15**	**14**	**50**	**55**	**54**
Arsenal	42	13	12	17	52	49	51
Sheffield Wednesday	42	13	12	17	49	57	51
West Ham United	42	13	11	18	44	48	50
Everton	42	11	17	14	44	51	50
Coventry City	42	12	14	16	44	62	50
Manchester City	42	12	13	17	53	64	49
Aston Villa	42	11	15	16	51	56	48
Crystal Palace	42	11	12	19	34	49	45
Norwich City	42	10	13	19	37	54	43
Leicester City	42	6	11	25	45	80	29
Ipswich Town	42	7	6	29	36	93	27

1995-96 SEASON

F.A. PREMIERSHIP

Manchester United	38	25	7	6	73	35	82
Newcastle United	38	24	6	8	66	37	78
Liverpool	38	20	11	7	70	34	71
Aston Villa	38	18	9	11	52	35	63
Arsenal	38	17	12	9	49	32	63
Everton	38	17	10	11	64	44	61
Blackburn Rovers	38	18	7	13	61	47	61
Tottenham Hotspur	38	16	13	9	50	38	61
Nottingham Forest	38	15	13	10	50	54	58
West Ham United	38	14	9	15	43	52	51
Chelsea	**38**	**12**	**14**	**12**	**46**	**44**	**50**
Middlesbrough	38	11	10	17	35	50	43
Leeds United	38	12	7	19	40	57	43
Wimbledon	38	10	11	17	55	70	41
Sheffield Wednesday	38	10	10	18	48	61	40
Coventry City	38	8	14	16	42	60	38
Southampton	38	9	11	18	34	52	38
Manchester City	38	9	11	18	33	58	38
Q.P.R.	38	9	6	23	38	57	33
Bolton Wanderers	38	8	5	25	39	71	29